Nick Vandome

Photoshop Elements 13

in easy steps

For Windows and Mac

4721800000799 0

In easy steps is an imprint of In Easy Steps Limited
16 Hamilton Terrace · Holly Walk · Leamington Spa
Warwickshire · United Kingdom · CV32 4LY
www.ineasysteps.com

Notice of Liability
Every effort has been made to ensure that this book contains accurate
and current information. However, In Easy Steps Limited and the
author shall not be liable for any loss or damage suffered by readers
as a result of any information contained herein.

Trademarks
Photoshop® is a registered trademark of Adobe Systems Incorporated.
All other trademarks are acknowledged as belonging to their
respective companies.

In Easy Steps Limited supports The Forest Stewardship Council (FSC),
the leading international forest certification organisation. All our titles
that are printed on Greenpeace approved FSC certified paper carry the
FSC logo.

MIX
Paper from
responsible sources
FSC® C020837
FSC
www.fsc.org

Printed and bound in the United Kingdom

ISBN 978-1-84078-640-8

Contents

1 **Introducing Elements** 7

About Elements 8
Welcome Screen 9
Photo Editor Workspace 10
Quick Edit Mode 12
Guided Edit Mode 13
Expert Edit Mode 14
Menu Bar 18
Preferences 19
Organizer Workspace 20
Create Mode 22
Share Mode 23
eLive 24
Getting Help 26

2 **Organizing Images** 27

Obtaining Images 28
Media View 30
Stacks 34
Version Sets 35
People View 36
Places View 38
Events View 40
Tagging Images 42
Searching for Images 44
Albums 48
Folders 49
Opening and Saving Images 50
Working with Video 51

3 First Digital Steps — 53

Color Enhancements	54
Cropping	57
Cloning	60
Pattern Cloning	61
Healing Brush	62
Spot Healing Brush	63
Rotating	64
Transforming	65
Magnification	66
Eraser	68

4 Quick Wins — 69

Removing Red-eye	70
Quickly Removing Items	72
Content-Aware Editing	74
Changing to Black and White	76
Quick Edit Mode Options	78
Quick Edit Toolbox	79
Quick Edit Adjustments	80
Enhancing with Quick Edits	82
Using Guided Edit Mode	84
Photomerge Effects	86
Photomerge Compose	88
Panoramas	90

5 Beyond the Basics — 93

Hue and Saturation	94
Histogram	96
Levels	98
Importing RAW Images	100
Image Size	102
Resampling Images	104

6 Selecting Areas — 105

About Selections	106
Marquee Tools	107
Lasso Tools	108

Magic Wand Tool 110
Selection Brush Tool 111
Quick Selection Tool 112
Smart Brush Tool 113
Inverting a Selection 114
Feathering 115
Refining Selections 116
Editing Selections 118

7 Layers 119

Layering Images 120
Layers Panel 121
Adding Layers 122
Fill and Adjustment Layers 123
Working with Layers 125
Layer Masks 126
Opacity 129
Saving Layers 130

8 Text and Drawing Tools 131

Adding and Formatting Text 132
Customizing Text 134
Distorting Text 138
Text and Shape Masks 139
Adding Shapes 141
Paint Bucket Tool 142
Gradient Tool 143
Brush and Pencil Tools 145
Impressionist Brush Tool 146
Working with Color 147

9 Artistic Effects 149

About Graphics and Effects 150
Adding Filters 152
Zoom Burst 154
Depth of Field 156
Photo Puzzles 158
Out of Bounds 160
Black and White Selection 163
Reflections 164

10 Sharing and Creating 167

About Share Mode   168
Mobile Sharing   170
Sharing with Adobe Revel   172
About Create Mode   173
Facebook Covers   177

11 Printing Images 179

Print Size   180
Print Functions   181
Print Layouts   183
Online Prints   185
Creating PDF Files   186

Index 187

1 Introducing Elements

Photoshop Elements is a digital image editing program that comprehensively spans the gap between very basic programs and professional-level ones. This chapter introduces the various workspaces and modes of Elements and shows how to access them and details what can be done with each one.

8 About Elements

9 Welcome Screen

10 Photo Editor Workspace

12 Quick Edit Mode

13 Guided Edit Mode

14 Expert Edit Mode

18 Menu Bar

19 Preferences

20 Organizer Workspace

22 Create Mode

23 Share Mode

24 eLive

26 Getting Help

About Elements

Photoshop Elements is the offspring of the professional-level image-editing program, Photoshop. Photoshop is somewhat unusual in the world of computer software, in that it is widely accepted as being the best program of its type on the market. If professional designers or photographers are using an image-editing program, it will almost certainly be Photoshop. However, two of the potential drawbacks to Photoshop are its cost and its complexity. This is where Elements comes into its own. Adobe (the maker of Photoshop and Elements) has recognized that the majority of digital imaging users (i.e. the consumer market) want something with the basic power of Photoshop, but with enough user-friendly features to make it easy to use. With the explosion in the digital camera market, a product was needed to meet the needs of a new generation of image editors – and that product is Elements.

Elements contains most of the same powerful editing/color management tools as the full version of Photoshop and it also includes a number of versatile features for sharing images and for creating artistic projects, such as slideshows, cards, calendars and online photo albums. It also has valuable features, such as the Guided edit and Quick edit modes, where you can quickly apply editing techniques and follow step-by-step processes to achieve a range of creative and artistic effects.

Special effects

One of the great things about using Elements with digital images is that it provides numerous fun and creative options for turning mediocre images into eye-catching works of art. This is achieved through a wide variety of guided activities within Guided edit mode, which have been added to and enhanced in Elements 13.

Advanced features

In addition to user-friendly features, Elements also has an Expert editing mode where you can use a range of advanced features, including a full set of tools for editing and color adjustments.

Photoshop Elements can be bought online from Adobe and computer and software sites, or at computer software stores. There are Windows and Mac versions of the program and with Elements 13 these are virtually identical. If Elements 13 is bought from the Adobe website, at **www.adobe.com**, it can be downloaded and installed directly from there. Otherwise it will be provided on a DVD, with a serial number that needs to be entered during installation.

The New icon pictured above indicates a new or enhanced feature introduced with the latest version of Photoshop Elements 13.

Welcome Screen

When you first open Elements, you will be presented with the Welcome Screen. This offers initial advice about working with Elements and also provides options for accessing the different workspaces. The Welcome Screen appears by default but this can be altered once you become more familiar with Elements.

Welcome Screen functions

1 Options for organizing photos, editing them and using them in a variety of creative ways

Hot tip

The Welcome Screen can be accessed at any time by selecting **Help > Welcome Screen** from the Photo Editor or Organizer Menu bar. Click on this button at the top of the Welcome Screen to select options for what happens when Elements is launched.

2 Click on the **Organizer** button to go to that area

3 Click on the **Photo Editor** button to go to that area

Photo Editor Workspace

From the Welcome Screen the Photo Editor workspace can be accessed. This is a combination of the work area (where images are opened and edited), menus, toolbars, toolboxes and panels. At first it can seem a little daunting, but Elements has been designed with three different editing modes to give you as many options as possible for editing your photos.

The components of the Photo Editor (Editor) are:

In Elements 13 there is an **eLive** button on the top toolbar too. This links to a range of help and news articles about Elements. See pages 24-25 for details.

Menu bar   Editor mode buttons   Panels bin

Toolbox   Taskbar   Work area

Editor modes

The three different modes in the Photo Editor are accessed from the buttons at the top of the Elements window. They are:

- **Quick edit mode.** This can be used to perform quick editing options in one step

- **Guided edit mode.** This can be used to perform a range of editing techniques in a step-by-step process for each

- **Expert edit mode.** This can be used for the ultimate control over the editing process

...cont'd

Taskbar and Tool Options

The Taskbar is the group of buttons that is available across all three Editor modes at the bottom left of the Elements window:

One of the options on the Taskbar is the Tool Options. This displays the available options for any tool selected from the Toolbox (different tools are available in each of the different Editor modes). To use this:

 Select a tool and click on the **Tool Options** button to show or hide the Tool Options panel (by default it is visible when a tool is first selected). Other tools within specific sets can also be selected within the Tool Options panel

Photo Bin

The Photo Bin is another feature that can be accessed from all three Editor modes. The Photo Bin enables you to quickly access all of the images that you have open within the Editor. To use the Photo Bin:

 Open two or more images. The most recently-opened one will be the one that is active in the Editor window

2 All open images are shown here in the Photo Bin

3 Double-click on an image in the Photo Bin to make that the active one for editing

Don't forget

The items on the Taskbar are, from left to right, show or hide the Photo Bin, show or hide the Tool Options panel, undo the previous actions, redo any undone actions, rotate the active photo and access the Organizer. In Expert mode there is also an option to change the Layout.

Hot tip

Images can also be made active for editing by dragging them directly from the Photo Bin and dropping them within the Editor window.

Hot tip

When an image has started to be edited, this icon appears on its top right-hand corner in the Photo Bin.

11

Quick Edit Mode

Quick edit mode contains a number of functions that can be selected from panels and applied to an image, without the need to manually apply all of the commands. To do this:

Don't forget

For a more detailed look at Quick edit mode, have a look at Chapter Four.

1 In the Editor, click on the **Quick** button

2 The currently-active image is displayed within the Quick edit window. This has the standard Taskbar and Photo Bin and a reduced Toolbox. Click here to access the Quick edit panels

Don't forget

Move the cursor over one of the thumbnails to view a real-time preview of the effect on the open image. Click on one of the thumbnails to apply the effect.

3 Select one of the commands to have it applied to the active image. This can be applied either by clicking on one of the thumbnail options or by dragging the appropriate slider at the top of the panel

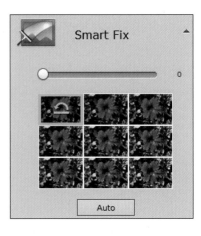

4 Click on these buttons at the bottom of the Quick Edit panel to select **Adjustments**, **Effects**, **Textures** and **Frames** options for adding to photos

Guided Edit Mode

Guided edit mode focuses on common tasks for editing digital images and shows you how to perform them with a step-by-step process. To use Guided edit mode:

1 In the Editor, click on the **Guided** button

2 The currently-active image is displayed within the Guided edit window. This has the standard Taskbar and Photo Bin but only two tools in the Toolbox. The Guided edit options are available in the right-hand panel

3 Select one of the actions that you want to perform. This will take you to a step-by-step process for undertaking the selected action

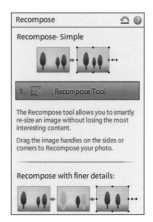

Don't forget

Guided edit mode is a great place to start if you are new to image editing, or feel unsure about anything to do with it.

Don't forget

The tools in the Guided edit mode Toolbox are the Zoom tool for magnifying an image and the Hand tool for moving around.

13

Expert Edit Mode

Expert edit mode is where you can take full editing control over your photos. It has a range of powerful editing tools so that you can produce subtle and impressive effects. To use Expert mode:

1 In the Editor, click on the **Expert** button

Expert

2 The full range of editing tools is available

Expert mode Toolbox   Open panels

The Organizer can be accessed from any of the Editor modes by clicking on this button on the Taskbar:

Organizer

Taskbar Layout button   Expert mode Panel buttons

The **Layout** button is the one addition on the Taskbar within Expert mode, as opposed to Quick and Guided edit modes. Click on the **Layout** button to access options for display of open photos within the Editor window.

Column and Rows
Rows and Column
All Grid
All Column
All Row
All Floating
Default

Layout

14

...cont'd

The Expert Toolbox

The Toolbox in Expert mode contains tools for applying a wide range of editing techniques. Some of the tools have more than one option. To see if a tool has additional options:

1 Move the cursor over the **Toolbox**. Tools that have additional options appear with a small arrow in the top right-hand corner of their icons. Click on a tool to view the options within the Tool Options panel

The tools that have additional options are: Marquee, Lasso, Quick Selection, Healing Brush, Type, Smart Brush, Eraser, Brush, Stamp, Shape, Blur and Sponge.

The default Toolbox tools are (keyboard shortcut in brackets):

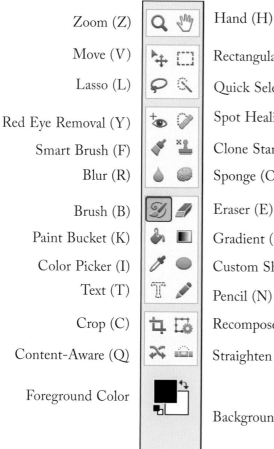

Zoom (Z) — Hand (H)
Move (V) — Rectangular Marquee (M)
Lasso (L) — Quick Selection (A)
Red Eye Removal (Y) — Spot Healing Brush (J)
Smart Brush (F) — Clone Stamp (S)
Blur (R) — Sponge (O)
Brush (B) — Eraser (E)
Paint Bucket (K) — Gradient (G)
Color Picker (I) — Custom Shape (U)
Text (T) — Pencil (N)
Crop (C) — Recompose (W)
Content-Aware (Q) — Straighten (K)
Foreground Color — Background Color

Keyboard shortcuts can be used by pressing the Shift key and the appropriate letter.

If the Toolbox is not visible, select **Window > Tools** from the Editor Menu bar.

15

Hot tip

The panels are located in the Panel Bin, which is at the right of the Editor window. In Expert edit mode this can be collapsed or expanded by selecting **Window > Panel Bin** from the Menu bar.

...cont'd

Panels

In Expert edit mode, Elements uses panels to group together similar editing functions and provide quick access to certain techniques. The available panels are:

- **Actions.** This can be used to perform automated actions over a group of images at the same time.

- **Adjustments.** This can be used to add or make editing changes to adjustment layers in the Layers panel.

- **Color Swatches.** This is a panel for selecting colors that can then be applied to parts of an image or elements that have been added to it.

- **Effects.** This contains special effects and styles that can be applied to an entire image or a selected part of an image. There are also filters which have their own dialog boxes in which settings can be applied and adjusted. Layer Styles can also be applied to elements within an image.

- **Favorites.** This is where favorite graphical elements from the Content panel can be stored and retrieved quickly.

- **Graphics.** This contains graphical elements that can be added to images, including backgrounds, frame shapes and text.

- **Histogram.** This displays a graph of the tonal range of the colors in an image. It is useful for assessing the overall exposure of an image and it changes as an image is edited.

- **History.** This can be used to undo any editing steps that have been performed. Every action is displayed and can be reversed by dragging the slider next to the most recent item.

- **Info.** This displays information about an image, or a selected element within it. This includes details about the color in an image or the position of a certain item.

- **Layers.** This enables several layers to be included within an image. This can be useful if you want to add elements to an existing image, such as shapes or text.

- **Navigator.** This can be used to move around an image and magnify certain areas of it.

...cont'd

Working with panels

The default Expert edit mode panels (Layers, Effects, Graphics and Favorites) are located at the right-hand side of the Taskbar. Additional panels can also be accessed from here. To work with panels in Expert edit mode:

1 Click on one of the panel buttons on the Taskbar to open the related panel

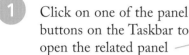

2 If there are additional tabs for a panel click on the tab to view the other options

Click here to access the menu for an open panel.

3 Click on the **More** button to view the rest of the available panels

Beware

Do not have too many panels open at one time. If you do, the screen will become cluttered and it will be difficult to edit images effectively.

4 The additional panels are grouped together. Click on a tab to access the required panel. Click and drag on a tab to move the panel away from the rest of the group

17

Don't forget

Although the Menu bar menus are all available in each of the Editor modes, some of the menu options are not available in Quick edit or Guided edit mode.

Beware

Elements does not support the CMYK color model for editing digital images. This could be an issue if you use a commercial printer.

Don't forget

The Mac version of Elements also has a Photoshop Elements menu on the Menu bar. This contains the Preferences options.

Menu Bar

In the Editor, the Menu bar contains menus that provide all of the functionality for the workings of Elements. Some of these functions can also be achieved through the use of the other components of Elements, such as the Toolbox, the Tool Options panel and the panels. However, the Menu bar is where all of the commands needed for the digital editing process can be accessed in one place.

Menu bar menus

- **File.** This has standard commands for opening, saving and printing images.

- **Edit.** This contains commands for undoing previous operations, and standard copy-and-paste techniques.

- **Image.** This contains commands for altering the size, shape and position of an image. It also contains more advanced functions, such as changing the color mode of an image.

- **Enhance.** This contains commands for editing the color elements of an image. It also contains quick-fix options and commands for creating Photomerge effects such as panoramas and combining exposures.

- **Layer.** This contains commands for working with different layers within an image.

- **Select.** This contains commands for working with areas that have been selected within an image, with one of the selection tools in the Toolbox.

- **Filter.** This contains numerous filters that can be used to apply special effects to an image.

- **View.** This contains commands for changing the size at which an image is displayed, and also options for showing or hiding rulers and grid lines.

- **Window.** This contains commands for changing the way multiple images are displayed, and also options for displaying the components of Elements.

- **Help.** This contains the various Help options.

Preferences

A number of preferences can be set within Elements to determine the way the program operates. It is perfectly acceptable to leave all of the default settings as they are, but as you become more familiar with the program you may want to change some of the preference settings. Preferences can be accessed by selecting **Edit > Preferences** from the Menu bar (**Adobe Photoshop Elements Editor > Preferences** in the Mac version). The available ones are:

- **General.** This contains a variety of options for selecting items, such as shortcut keys.

- **Saving Files.** This determines the way Elements saves files.

- **Performance.** This determines how Elements allocates memory when processing editing tasks. It also determines how Elements allocates disk space when processing editing tasks (scratch disks). If you require more memory for editing images you can do this by allocating up to four scratch disks on your hard drive. These act as extra areas from which memory can be used during the editing process.

- **Display & Cursors.** This determines how cursors operate when certain tools are selected.

- **Transparency.** This determines the color, or transparency, of the background on which an open image resides.

- **Units & Rulers.** This determines the unit of measurement used by items, such as rulers.

- **Guides & Grids.** This determines the color and format of any guides and grids that are used.

- **Plug-Ins.** This displays any plug-ins that have been downloaded to enhance image editing with Elements.

- **Type.** This determines the way text appears when it is added to images.

- **Organize & Share.** These preferences open in Organizer mode and offer a collection of options for each function. These are General, Files, Editing, Camera or Card Reader, Scanner, Keyword Tags and Albums, Sharing, Adobe Sharing Services, Media-Analysis and Adobe Revel for online sharing.

Each preference has its own dialog box in which the specific preference settings can be made.

A scratch disk is an area of temporary storage on the hard drive that can be utilized if the available memory (RAM) has been used up.

Guides and grids can be accessed from the View menu in Editor mode.

Organizer Workspace

The Organizer workspace contains functions for sorting, viewing and finding multiple images. To use the Organizer:

 In any of the Editor modes, click on the **Organizer** button on the Taskbar

The Organizer has four views, in addition to eLive, accessed from these buttons:

- Media View   **Media**
- People View   **People**
- Places View   **Places**
- Events View   **Events**

Media View

The Media View displays thumbnails of your photos, and also has functions for sorting and finding images:

Folders and Albums   View buttons   Thumbnails

Organizer Taskbar   Instant Fix and Tag/Info buttons

Click on these buttons to apply image-editing effects to a selected image in Media View, or view the Tags and Information panels.

People View

This view can be used to tag specific people and then view photos with those people in them.

Don't forget

For information about using the Organizer, and its different views, see Chapter Two.

Places View

This view can be used to place photos on a map so that they can be searched for by location.

Events View

This view can be used to group photos according to specific events such as birthdays and vacations.

21

Create Mode

Create mode is where you can release your artistic flair and start designing items such as photo books and photo collages. It can also be used to create slide shows and to put your images onto discs. To use Create mode:

Don't forget

For a more detailed look at Create mode have a look at pages 173-176.

 In either the Editor or the Organizer, click on the **Create** button

 Select one of the Create projects. Each project has a wizard that takes you through the create process

The Create wizard takes you through the process so you can display your photos in a variety of creative ways

Share Mode

Share mode can be used to distribute your images to family and friends in a number of creative ways. To use Share mode:

1 In the Organizer, click on the **Share** button

2 Select one of the Share options, such as sharing to social networking sites, sharing via email or the Adobe Revel photo-sharing service which is accessed through the Private Web Album option

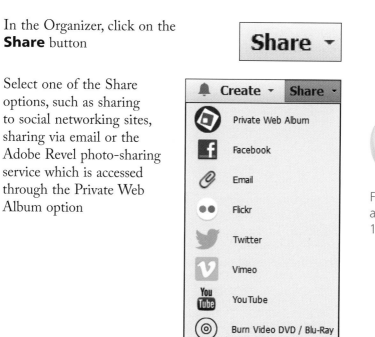

For a more detailed look at Share mode see pages 168-172.

3 In previous versions of Elements, the Share function was only available from the Organizer. However, in Elements 13 there are also some share options that can be accessed from the Editor

eLive

eLive is a new function in Elements 13 and it provides a selection of tutorials and videos for getting the most out of Elements. To access these, click on the eLive button on the top toolbar in either Editor or Organizer mode.

eLive

Menu options

There are three sections with eLive, Inspire, Learn and News:

1 Click on this button to view the menu options

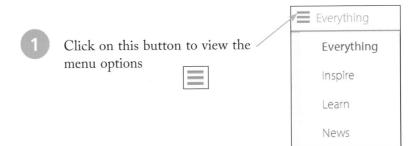

Inspire

The Inspire section provides details of how you can get more out of your photos:

1 Click on the **Inspire** button from the main menu to view the options

2 Click on one of the items to see more details. This links to a selection of online resources including, for Inspire, the Elements Facebook page

Learn

The Learn section provides details of how you can learn a range of photo editing techniques:

 Click on the **Learn** button from the main menu to view the options

 Click on one of the items to see more details. This links to a selection of online resources including, for Learn, the Elements YouTube page

Hot tip

If there are any updates to the eLive resources, this is indicated by a red icon with a number in it, on the eLive button.

News

The News section provides details of how you can keep up-to-date with the latest news about Elements.

Click on the **News** button from the main menu to view the options

Click on one of the items to see more details. For News, this takes you to the Adobe website

Getting Help

One of the differences between Elements and the full version of Photoshop is the amount of assistance and guidance offered by each program. Since Photoshop is aimed more at the professional end of the market, the level of help is confined largely to the standard help directory that serves as an online manual. Elements also contains this, but in addition it has the Getting Started option which is designed to take users through the digital image editing process as smoothly as possible. The Getting Started option offers general guidance about digital imaging techniques and there are also help items that can be accessed by selecting Help from the Menu bar. These include online help, information on available plug-ins for Elements, tutorials and support details.

Using the help files

 Select **Photoshop Elements Help** from the **Help** menu and click on an item to display it in the main window. Use the left-hand panel to view the different help categories

| ≡ MENU   Q SEARCH   NICK   Adobe |

Learn & Support / Photoshop Elements Help

Adobe Community Help

Q Search	Getting Started tutorials	Selecting	Printing, sharing, and exporting
	What's new	Color	Photo projects
	Workspace and workflows	Drawing and painting	Web graphics
Help for previous versions	Importing	Effects and filters	Keyboard shortcuts
	File management	Text and shapes	
System requirements	Editing photos	Layers	

Getting Started tutorials — To the top

Getting started tutorials — Learn Photoshop Elements video tutorials

What's new — To the top

What's new in Photoshop Elements 13 — Elements Organizer 13 manual (PDF)
What's new in Elements Organizer 13 — What's new in Photoshop Elements 12
Photoshop Elements 13 manual (PDF) — What's new in Elements Organizer 12

Community Forums

Workspace and workflows More — To the top

Workspace basics — Rulers, grids, and guides
Panels and bins — Undo, redo, and cancel actions
Tools — Scratch disks, plug-ins, and application updates

2 Organizing Images

This chapter shows how to download digital images via Elements and then how to view and organize them, including using the People, Places and Events views. It shows how you can tag images, so that they are easy to find, and how to search for items according to a variety of criteria and also using albums and folders.

28 **Obtaining Images**

30 **Media View**

34 **Stacks**

35 **Version Sets**

36 **People View**

38 **Places View**

40 **Events View**

42 **Tagging Images**

44 **Searching for Images**

48 **Albums**

49 **Folders**

50 **Opening and Saving Images**

51 **Working with Video**

Obtaining Images

One of the first tasks in Elements is to import images so that you can start editing and sharing them. This can be done from a variety of devices, but the process is similar for all of them. To import images into Elements:

Don't forget

For many digital cameras, the Photo Downloader window will appear automatically once the camera is connected to the computer. However, if this does not happen it will have to be accessed manually as shown here.

Hot tip

Images can also be imported from existing files and folders on a computer. This means that they will be added to the Organizer's database and you will be able to apply all of its features to the images.

 Access the **Organizer** by clicking on this button in the Editor

 Select **File > Get Photos and Videos** from the Menu bar and select the type of device from which you want to load images into Elements, or

From **F**iles and Folders...	Ctrl+Shift+G
From **C**amera or Card Reader...	Ctrl+G
From **S**canner...	Ctrl+U
By S**e**arching...	

3 Click on the **Import** button and select one of the options for obtaining images

4 If you select **From Camera or Card Reader**, click under **Get Photos from** to select a specific device

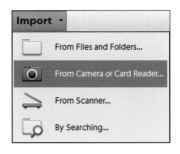

Get Photos from:

-- Select a Device --

N E:\<NIKON D70>
I:\<LEXAR>
< Refresh List >
-- Select a Device --

5 The images to be downloaded are displayed here, next to the device from which they will be downloaded

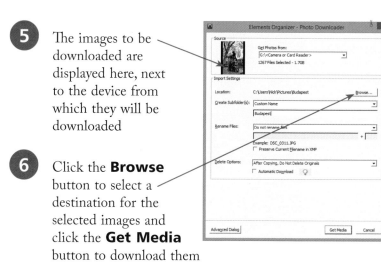

6 Click the **Browse** button to select a destination for the selected images and click the **Get Media** button to download them

7 Click on the **Advanced Dialog** button to access additional options for downloading your images. Here you can select specific images so that they are not all downloaded at once

8 Click on the **Get Media** button so that the images are imported. They can then be viewed in the Organizer and opened in the Editor

Hot tip

Images can also be downloaded from a pen drive. To do this, connect the pen drive and use the **From Camera or Card Reader** download option. You will then be able to download the images in the same way as with a camera or card reader.

29

Copying - 14% Completed

From: **G:\<Camera or Card Reader>**
To: C:\Users\Nick\Pictures\Budapest

14%

File 39 of 256: Copying File...

DSC_0274.JPG

Minimize   Stop

Media View

The Media View is the function within the Organizer that is used to view, find and sort images. When using the Media View, images have to be actively added to it so it can then catalog them. Once images have been imported, the Media View acts as a window for viewing and sorting your images, no matter where they are located. Media View is the default view when you access the Organizer and can be accessed at any time by clicking on the Media button:

The Media View can be set to watch specific folders on your computer. Whenever images are added to these folders, or edited within them, you will be prompted to add them into the Media View. To specify folders to be watched, select **File > Watch Folders** from the Menu bar and then browse to the folder, or folders, that you want to include. This ensures that images in different locations will still be updated by the Media View.

Folders and Albums   Tag and Info panels

Organizer Taskbar   Instant Fix and Tag/Info buttons

The Media View can also be used to display video files, audio files, Elements' projects and PDF files.

There is a magnification slider on the Taskbar that can be used for changing the size at which images are viewed in the main Media View window:

Accessing images

To access images within the Media View:

1 Click on images to select them individually, or as a group

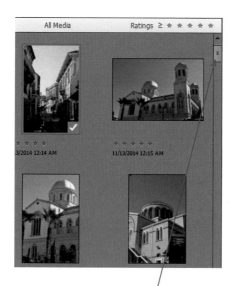

Hot tip

To select multiple images, drag around the thumbnails, or hold down **Shift** and click on a range of thumbnails to select them all. Or, hold down **Ctrl** (**Cmd** on a Mac) and click on thumbnails to select a group of non-consecutive images.

2 Drag here to scroll through images within the main window

3 Double-click on an image to view it in the whole Media View window

Hot tip

If images were captured with a digital camera they will appear in the Media View on the date the image was taken. To make sure this is accurate, set your camera to the correct date and time.

31

...cont'd

Media View functionality

The Media View has a considerable amount of power and functionality in terms of organizing and editing images within the Organizer. This includes the Taskbar and panels for adding tags to images and viewing information about them:

 The Taskbar is located at the bottom of the main window and contains buttons for, from left to right, show or hide the Albums and Folders panel, undo the previous action, rotate a selected image, tag people for People View, add images to a map for Places View, add an event to images for Event View, view the selected images in a slideshow, access the selected image in the Editor and mark faces

If you use the Slideshow option and do not select any images, the whole catalog will be used for the slideshow.

 At the right-hand side of the Taskbar, use these buttons to apply editing fixes to a selected image and access the **Tags** and **Information** panels

 Select an image in the main Media View window and click on this button to apply instant editing fixes to it (without having to move to the Editor)

Click on one of the editing functions to apply it to the select image(s)

...cont'd

 5 Click on this button to view details of selected images in Media View

 6 Click on the **Information** tab. Click on these arrows to expand each section

Tags	Information
▸ General	
▸ Metadata	
▸ History	

For more details about adding tags to images see pages 42-43.

 7 Access the **General** panel to see information about the image name, size, date taken and where it is saved on your computer. You can edit the name and add a caption here

Tags	Information
▾ General	

Caption: Limassol
Name: DSC_0913.JPG
Notes:
Ratings: ☆ ☆ ☆ ☆ ☆
Size: 5.2MB 3072x4608
Date: 11/13/2014 12:14 AM
Location: C:\Users\Nick\Pictures\Cyprus\
Audio: <none>

A caption can also be added to an image by selecting it and selecting **Edit > Add Caption** from the Menu bar.

 8 Access the **Metadata** panel to see detailed information about an image that is added by the camera when it is taken

▾ Metadata
▾ FILE PROPERTIES
Filename: DSC_0913.JPG
Document Type: image/jpeg
Date Created: 11/17/2014 4:24 P
Date Modified: 11/13/2014 12:14
▾ CAMERA DATA (EXIF)
Make: NIKON CORPORAT
Model: NIKON D3100
ISO Speed Ratings: 200
Exposure Time: 1/200 sec
F-Stop: f/13
Focal Len...5mm Film: 69
Focal Length: 46.00 mm
Flash: Did not fire

9 Click on this button to view an expanded list of metadata information

10 Access the **History** panel to view the editing history of the image

▾ History
Modified Date: 11/13/2014 12:14 AM
Imported On: 11/25/2014
Imported From: hard disk
Volume Name: Acer

33

Stacks

Since digital cameras make it quick, easy and cheap to capture dozens, or hundreds, of images on a single memory card it is no surprise that most people are now capturing more images than ever before. One result of this is that it is increasingly tempting to take several shots of the same subject, just to try to capture the perfect image. The one drawback with this is that when it comes to organizing your images on a computer it can become time-consuming to work your way through all of your near-identical shots. The Media View offers a useful solution to this by allowing you to stack similar images, so that you can view a single thumbnail rather than several. To do this:

Beware

You can remove images from a stack by selecting the stack in the Media View and selecting **Edit > Stack > Flatten Stack** from the Menu bar. However, this will remove all of the images, apart from the top one, from the Media View. This does not remove them from your hard drive, although there is an option to do this too, if you wish.

Don't forget

To revert stacked images to their original state, select the stack and select **Edit > Stack > Unstack Photos** from the Menu bar.

 Select the images that you want to stack in the Media View

 Select **Edit > Stack > Stack Selected Photos** from the Menu bar

 The images are stacked into a single thumbnail and the existence of the stack is indicated by this icon

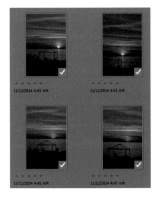

 To view all of the stacked images, click here

5 Click here to return to all of the photos in the Media View

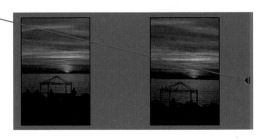

Version Sets

When working with digital images it is commonplace to create several different versions from a single image. This could be to use one for printing and one for use on the Web, or because there are elements of an image that you want to edit. Instead of losing track of images that have been edited it is possible to create stacked thumbnails of edited images, which are known as version sets. These can include the original image and all of the edited versions. Version sets can be created and added to from the Photo Editor and viewed in Media View. To do this:

 Open an image in the Photo Editor

 Make editing changes to the image in either Expert edit mode or Quick edit mode

 Select **File > Save As** from the Menu bar

The other version set menu options include **Flatten Version Set**, and **Revert to Original**. The latter deletes all of the other versions except the original image.

Check on the **Save in Version Set with Original** box and click **Save**

 In Media View, the original image and the edited one are grouped together in a stack, and the fact that it is a version set is denoted next to the set

 To view all of the images in a version set, select the set and select **Edit > Version Set > Expand Items in Version Set** from the Menu bar

People View

People shots are popular in most types of photography. However, this can result in hundreds, or thousands, of photos of different people. In Elements there is a feature that enables you to tag people throughout your collections. This is known as people recognition. To use this:

1 In Media View of the Organizer, either select individual images, or do not select any to have people recognition applied to the whole collection. Click on the **Add People** button on the Taskbar

2 The Organizer will analyze each photo and display a prompt box for each new face it finds

3 Enter a name in the prompt box. Other similar photos will have this name added to them too

Adding people manually

To add people's names manually:

1 Open a photo at full size in the Media View and click on the **Mark Face** button

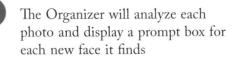

2 A prompt box appears on the screen. Drag this over the required face, add a name in the **Who is this?** box and click on the green tick to apply the name

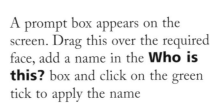

Viewing people

To view people who have been tagged with people recognition:

 1 Click on the **People** button in the main Organizer window

Although people recognition is very accurate, it may, at times, identify objects that are not faces at all.

2 The people photos are stacked in a thumbnail. Double-click on the thumbnail to view all of the photos

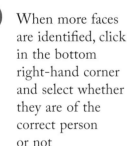

3 To add more photos with the selected person, click on the **Find More** button on the People View Taskbar

Find More

People recognition really comes into its own when you have tagged dozens, or hundreds, of photos. You can then view all of the photos containing a specific person.

4 When more faces are identified, click in the bottom right-hand corner and select whether they are of the correct person or not

5 Click on the **Save** button

Save

37

Places View

One of the most common reasons for taking photos is when people are on vacation in different and new locations. Within the Organizer it is possible to tag photos to specific locations on a map, so that you can quickly view all of your photos from a certain area. To do this:

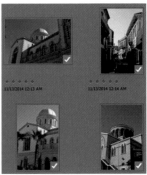

 In Media View, select all of the photos from a specific location

 On the Taskbar, click on the **Add Places** button

3 The Places View window opens with the selected photos in the top panel and a map in the main panel

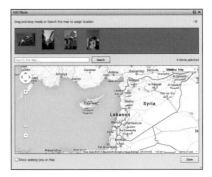

 Use these controls to move around the map and zoom in and out on it

Hot tip

You can also move around the map by clicking and dragging. You can also zoom in and out by right-clicking on the map and selecting the relevant command.

5 Drag the photos onto a specific location on the map to tag them at this point. Click here to confirm the action

6 A red flag is placed on the map at the point where the photos were placed. The number of tagged photos is indicated on the flag

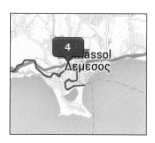

7 Click on the **Done** button

8 To view photos that have been placed on a map, click on the **Places** button in the main Organizer window

9 Red markers indicate all of the locations at which photos have been placed. All photos are shown in the left-hand panel

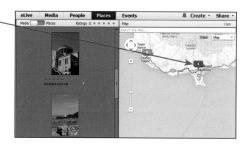

Beware

10 Click on an arrow and click on the **Show Media** button to view the photos just for this location

11 Click on the **Add Places** button to add photos to another location

If a photo with an existing location is selected and the Add Places button is clicked, the location for the photo can be changed, but it will be removed from the original one.

Events View

Photos in the Organizer can also be allocated to specific events such as family celebrations or overseas trips. This is done with the Events View. To do this:

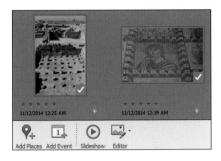

1 In Media View, select all of the required photos for a specific event

2 On the Taskbar, click on the **Add Event** button

3 In the Add New Event panel, add details including name, start and end date and a description of the event

4 Click on the **Done** button

5 To view photos that have been allocated to an event, click on the **Events** button in the main Organizer window

6 All photos for a specific event are grouped together

Hot tip

Click on the 'i' icon on the thumbnail in the Events window to see the description for that particular event.

7 Double-click on the thumbnail to view all of the photos allocated to the event

8 Click on the **Back** button to go back to the thumbnail view in Step 6

9 Click on the **Calendar** to view events from specific dates

10 Click on the **Add Event** button to create another event in Event View. This is done by dragging photos into the media bin and entering the event details as in Step 3

Tagging Images

As your digital image collection begins to grow on your computer it is increasingly important to be able to keep track of your images and find the ones you want, when you want them. One way of doing this is by assigning specific tags to images. You can then search for images according to the tags that have been added to them. The tagging function is accessed from the Tags panel within the Media View in the Organizer. To add tags to images:

42

Hot tip

When you create a new category you can also choose a new icon.

1 In Media View, click on this button on the Taskbar to show and hide the Tags panel

Tags/Info

2 Click here to access the currently-available tags

3 Click here to access sub-categories for a particular category

Tags	Information
▼ Keywords	+▾

- ☐ 🏷 Nature
- ▸ ☐ 🏷 Color
- ☐ 🏷 Photography
- ☐ 🏷 Other

▸ People Tags   +▾
▸ Places Tags   +▾
▸ Events Tags   +▾

4 Click here to add categories, or sub-categories, of your own choice

Tags	Information	
▼ Keywords	+▾	

- ☐ 🏷 Nature
- ☐ 🏷 Color
- ☐ 🏷 Photography
- ☐ 🏷 Other

▸ People Tags
▸ Places Tags
▸ Events Tags

New Keyword Tag...	Ctrl+N
New Sub-Category...	
New Category...	
Edit...	
Import Keyword Tags from File...	
Save Keyword Tags to File...	
Collapse All Keyword Tags	
Expand All Keyword Tags	
Show Large Icon	

5 Enter a name for the new category, or sub-category, and click on the **OK** button

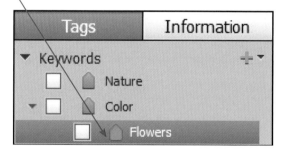

> Create Sub-Category
>
> Sub-Category Name
> Flowers
>
> Parent Category or Sub-Category
> Color ▼
>
> OK   Cancel

Hot tip

Multiple tags can be added to the same image. This gives you greater flexibility when searching for images.

6 Select the required images in the Media View

7 Drag a tag onto one of the selected images

Tags	Information

▼ Keywords   ╋ ▼
   ☐ 🏠 Nature
▼ ☐ 🏠 Color
      ☐ 🏠 Flowers

8 The tag will apply to all of the selected images. Each individual image will have the tag added to it

Don't forget

Tagged images can still be searched for by using a sub-category tag, even though they are denoted in the Media View by the tag for the main category.

9 The images are tagged with the icon that denotes the main category, rather than the sub-category

43

Searching for Images

Once images have been tagged they can be searched for using their tags. To do this:

Using the Search box
Images can be searched for simply by typing keywords into the Search box at the top of the Organizer, in any view:

 Click in the Search box

 Enter a keyword. As you type, suggestions will appear, including items that have been added to People View, Places View and Events View

 Click on one of the results to view all of the tagged images

Click on the **Sort By** box in Step 4 to sort the search results according to Newest, Oldest or Import Batch.

 Click on the **Back** button to go back to all images

Click here in the Search box to access other search options

Visual Similarity Search
Object Search
Duplicate Photo Search
Saved Searches

44

...cont'd

Searching with tags

Images can also be searched for using the tags within the Tags panel. To do this:

1 Access the Tags panel from this button

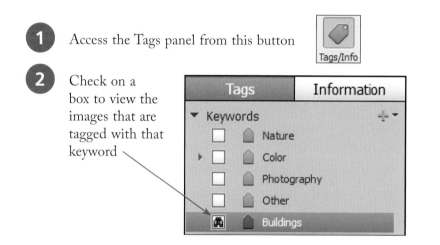

2 Check on a box to view the images that are tagged with that keyword

3 All matching items for a search are shown together within the Media View window

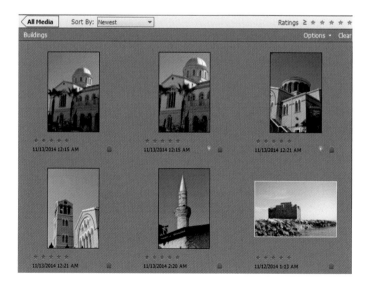

4 Click on the **All Media** button to return to the rest of the images

...cont'd

Multiple searches

Within the Tags panel it is also possible to define searches for images that have multiple (i.e. two or more) tags attached to them. To do this:

 Add a tag to an image, or images and click on the tag in the Tags panel to display all of 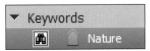 these images (other tags that have been added to them will also be displayed next to the image)

Hot tip

Images that have been tagged within People View, Places View and Events View can also be search for using the Keywords panel.

2 Add another tag to the image, or images, so that there are at least two attached. Click on both of these in the Tags panel. Only the  images containing both tags will be displayed

Searching by objects

In Elements it is also possible to search for images based on specific objects. For instance, you can search for images with a particular building, landscape or animal. To do this:

 Open an image that contains the object that you want to use for the search criteria

Two other search options are for **Visual Similarity** and **Duplicate Photos**. These display similar photos that can then be selected and placed in stacks for easier storage. It also enables you to look at similar photos and delete any that you don't want to keep.

Click on the down arrow next to the Search box and select the **Object Search** option

Drag the markers of the box over the object to resize it, or click and drag inside it to move the whole box

Click on the **Search Object** button

Drag this slider to refine the search according to Color or Shape.

Images with similar objects are displayed, with a percentage rating of how close the object match is

Albums

Albums in Elements are similar to physical photo albums: they are a location into which you can store all of your favorite groups of images. Once they have been stored there they can easily be found when required. To create albums:

Don't forget

Version Sets and Stacks can be added to, and viewed in, Albums.

 In the Media View, click here in the Albums panel and select **New Album**

 Enter a name for the new album

 Select the images that you would like included in the new album and drag them into the Content panel

 Click on the **OK** button

The selected images are placed into the new album. Click on an album to view the images within it

Folders

One important factor in storing and searching for photos is the use of folders. Elements can replicate the folder structure that you have on your hard drive and also create new folders and edit existing ones. To work with folders in Elements:

1 The available folders are listed next to the Albums section. Click on a folder to view its contents

Even if you import a single photo, the related folder will be created within Elements, containing the photo.

2 New folders are created whenever you import photos into Elements using the **Import > From Files and Folders** command

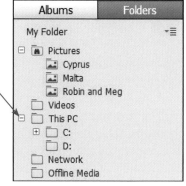

3 Click on this button to view the folder hierarchy as it is on your hard drive

Albums	Folders
My Folder	

- Pictures
  - Cyprus
  - Malta
  - Robin and Meg
- Videos
- This PC
  - C:
  - D:
- Network
- Offline Media

Right-click within the hierarchy view to add a new folder. When this is completed it also appears within your file structure on your computer's hard drive.

4 In hierarchy view, right-click on a folder to access the available options for editing it or adding a new folder

Reveal in Explorer
Add to Watched Folders
Import Media

New Folder
Rename Folder
Delete Folder

Create an Instant Album

Show All SubFolders

Another option for opening files is the **Open Recently Edited File** command, which is accessed from the File menu. This lists, in order, the files you have opened most recently. Some of these are also listed on the **Open** button.

A proprietary file format is one that is specific to the program being used. It has greater flexibility when used within the program itself but cannot be distributed as easily other images.

The **Save As** command should be used if you want to make a copy of an image with a different file name.

Opening and Saving Images

Once you have captured images with a digital camera, or a scanner, and stored them on your computer, you can open them in any of the Editor modes. There are a number of options for this:

Open command

 Select **File > Open** from the Menu bar or click on the **Open** button and select an option

 Select an image from your hard drive and click **Open**

Open As command

This can be used to open a file in a different file format from its original format. To do this:

 Select **File > Open As** from the Menu bar

 Select an image and select the file format. Click **Open**

Saving images

When saving digital images, it is always a good idea to save them in at least two different file formats, particularly if layered objects, such as text and shapes, have been added. One of these formats should be the proprietary Photoshop format PSD or PDD. The reason for using this is that it will retain all of the layered information within an image. So, if a text layer has been added, it will still be available for editing, once it has been saved and closed.

The other format that an image should be saved in, is the one most appropriate for the use to which it is going to be put. Therefore, images that are going to be used on the Web should be saved as JPEG, GIF or PNG files, while an image that is going to be used for printing should be saved in another format, such as TIFF. Once images have been saved in these formats, all of the layered information within them becomes flattened into a single layer and it will not be possible to edit this.

Working with Video

As well as using Elements for viewing and organizing photos, it can also be used in the same way with video. Video can be imported into Elements in a number of ways:

- From a camera that has video recording capabilities

- From a digital video camera

- From a cell/mobile phone

- From video that has been created in the Elements Premiere program. This is a companion program to Elements and is used to manipulate and edit video. It can be bought in a package with Elements, or individually. For more details see **www.adobe.com/products/premiere-elements/**

To download video into Elements:

 Connect the device containing the video. In the Organizer, click on the **Import** button, select the required device and download in the same way as for photos

Video clips are identified by this symbol on their thumbnail in Media View in the Organizer

The video is downloaded and displayed in the Organizer in the same way as photos

Don't forget

Elements Premiere can be bought as a package with Elements, or it can be bought individually.

Beware

Video files are usually much larger in size than photos, and if you have lots of them they will take up a lot of space on your computer.

...cont'd

Viewing video
To view video clips:

 Double-click on the clip in the Media View. The Elements video player will open and play the video clip

 Use the controls underneath the video window to navigate through the clip and adjust the volume

The **Find > By Media Type** option can also be used to find audio files, projects and PDFs.

Finding video
To find video clips within Elements:

 In the Organizer, select **Find > By Media Type > Video** from the Menu bar

3 First Digital Steps

This chapter shows how to get up and running with digital image editing, and details some effective editing techniques for improving digital images, such as improving the overall color and changing the size and shape of images.

54 Color Enhancements

57 Cropping

60 Cloning

61 Pattern Cloning

62 Healing Brush

63 Spot Healing Brush

64 Rotating

65 Transforming

66 Magnification

68 Eraser

Another Auto command on the Enhance menu is Auto Smart Fix. This can be used to automatically edit all of the color balance of an image in one step. This is also available as a panel in Quick edit mode.

Two other options for color enhancement are the Burn tool and the Dodge tool in the Toolbox. The Burn tool can be dragged over areas in an image to make them darker and the Dodge tool can be dragged over areas to make them lighter.

Color Enhancements

Some of the simplest, but most effective, editing changes that can be made to digital images are color enhancements. These can help to transform a mundane image into a stunning one, and Elements offers a variety of methods for achieving this. Some of these are verging towards the professional end of image editing, while others are done almost automatically by Elements. These are known as Auto adjustments and some simple manual adjustments can also be made to the brightness and contrast of an image. All of these color enhancement features can be accessed from the Enhance menu on the Menu bar in Expert and Quick edit modes.

Auto Levels

This automatically adjusts the overall color tone in an image in relation to the lightest and darkest points in the image:

Auto Contrast

This automatically adjusts the contrast in an image:

...cont'd

Auto Color Correction

This automatically adjusts all the color elements within an image:

Adjust Brightness/Contrast

This can be used to manually adjust the brightness and contrast in an image:

Apply small amounts of Brightness and Contrast at a time when you are editing an image. This will help ensure that the end result does not look too unnatural.

1 Select **Enhance > Adjust Lighting > Brightness/Contrast** from the Menu bar (in either Expert or Quick edit mode)

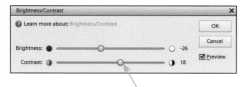

2 Drag the sliders to adjust the image brightness and contrast

3 Click on the **OK** button

4 The brightness and contrast (and a range of other color editing functions) can also be adjusted using the panels in Quick edit mode

Always make sure that the Preview box is checked when you are applying color enhancements. This will display the changes as you make them and before they are applied to the image.

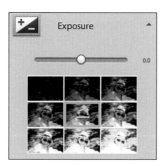

...cont'd

Adjust Shadows/Highlights

One problem that most photographers encounter at some point, is where part of an image is exposed correctly while another part is either over- or under-exposed. If this is corrected using general color correction techniques, such as levels or brightness and contrast, the poorly-exposed area may be improved, but at the expense of the area that was correctly exposed initially. To overcome this, the Shadows/Highlights command can be used to adjust particular tonal areas of an image. To do this:

Hot tip

Adjusting shadows can make a significant improvement to an image in which one area is underexposed and the rest is correctly exposed.

1 Open an image where parts of the image, or all of it, are incorrectly exposed

2 Select **Enhance > Adjust Lighting > Shadows/ Highlights** from the Menu bar

3 Make the required adjustments by dragging the sliders

4 Click on the **OK** button

5 The poorly-exposed areas of the image have been corrected

Cropping

Cropping is a technique that can be used to remove unwanted areas of an image and highlight the main subject. The area to be cropped can only be selected as a rectangle. To crop an image:

 Select the **Crop** tool from the Toolbox

 Click and drag on an image to select the area to be cropped. The area that is selected is retained and the area to be cropped appears grayed-out

The Tool Options for the Crop tool has an option for selecting pre-set sizes for the crop tool. This results in the crop being in specific proportions. For instance, if you want to print an image at 10 x 8 size, you can use this pre-set crop size to ensure that the cropped image has the correct proportions. The image dialog box will also be updated accordingly.

57

3 Click and drag on these markers to resize the crop area

4 Click on the check mark to accept the changes, or the circle to reject them

58

...cont'd

Overlay crop options

When performing cropping it is also possible to use various overlay grids to help the composition of the image. One of these is the Rule of Thirds. This is a photographic technique where a nine-segment grid is used to position elements within the image. Generally, the items that you want to give the most prominence to should be positioned at one of the intersections of the lines. To use the Rule of Thirds grid:

 Select the **Crop** tool and click on the **Rule of Thirds** button in the Tool Options panel

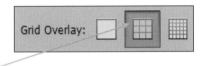

 Crop the image so that at least one of the main subjects is located at the intersections of the lines in grid. This can be in the foreground or the background

3 The image is cropped according to the Rule of Thirds grid

...cont'd

Auto Crop

To simplify the crop function, Elements 13 also has a range of auto crop options, where the suggested crop area is displayed using a range of preset options. To use these:

1 Select the **Crop** tool. The auto crop options are displayed on four buttons in the Tool Options panel

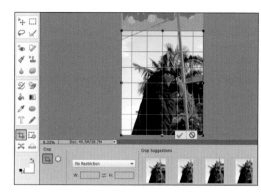

2 Move the cursor over one of the options to view the auto crop selection

Images can also be cropped using a larger grid. This can be useful if you are trying to align items within an image.

3 The auto crop selection is shown in the main window. Click on the green arrow to accept the suggested crop area, or click on the red circle to reject the suggestion

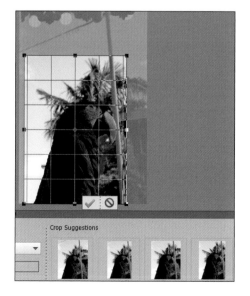

Cloning

Cloning is a technique that can be used to copy one area of an image over another. This can be used to cover up small imperfections in an image, such as a dust mark or a spot, and also to copy or remove large items in an image, such as a person.

To clone items:

60

1 Select the **Clone Stamp** tool from the Toolbox

2 Set the Clone Stamp options in the Tool Options panel

3 Hold down Alt and click on the image to select a source point from which the cloning will start

4 Drag the cursor to copy everything over which the selection point marker passes

Pattern Cloning

The Pattern Stamp tool can be used to copy a selected pattern over an image, or a selected area of an image. To do this:

1 Select the **Pattern Stamp** tool from the Toolbox

2 Click here in the Tool Options panel to access the available patterns

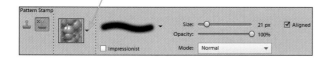

3 Select a pattern for the Pattern Stamp tool

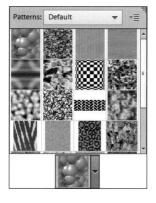

4 Click and drag on an image to copy the selected pattern over it

Don't forget

The Pattern Stamp tool is grouped in the Toolbox with the Clone Stamp tool. It can be selected from the Tool Options panel if the Clone Stamp tool is selected.

Hot tip

Patterns can be added to the patterns panel by selecting an image, or an area of an image, and selecting **Edit > Define Pattern** from the Editor Menu bar. Then give the pattern a name in the **Pattern Name** dialog box and click **OK**.

Healing Brush

One of the favorite techniques in digital imaging is removing unwanted items, particularly physical blemishes, such as spots and wrinkles. This can be done with the Clone tool but the effects can sometimes be too harsh, as a single area is copied over the affected item. A more subtle effect can be achieved with the Healing Brush and the Spot Healing Brush tools. The Healing Brush can be used to remove blemishes over larger areas, such as wrinkles:

Hot tip

The Healing Brush tool can be more subtle than the Clone tool, as it blends the copied area together with the area over which it is copying. This is particularly effective on people, as it preserves the overall skin tone better than the Clone tool does.

1 Open an image with blemishes covering a reasonably large area, i.e. more than a single spot

2 Select the **Healing Brush** tool from the Toolbox and make the required selections in the Tool Options panel

3 Hold down **Alt** and click on an area of the image to load the Healing Brush tool. Drag over the affected area. The cross is the area which is copied beneath the circle. At this point the overall tone is not perfect and looks too pink

4 Release the mouse and the Healing Brush blends the affected area with the one that was copied over it. This creates a much more natural skin tone

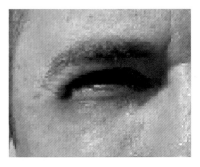

Spot Healing Brush

The Spot Healing Brush is very effective for quickly removing small blemishes in an image, such as spots. To do this:

1 Open an image and zoom in on the area with the blemish

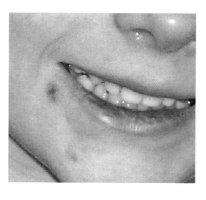

2 Select the **Spot Healing Brush** tool from the Toolbox and make the required selections in the Tool Options panel

Hot tip

When dragging over a blemish with the Spot Healing Brush tool, make sure the brush size is larger than the area of the blemish. This will ensure that you can cover the blemish in a single stroke.

3 Drag the Spot Healing Brush tool over the affected area

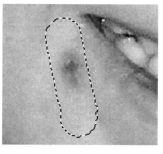

4 The blemish is removed and the overall skin tone is retained

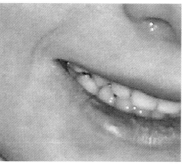

Rotating

Various rotation commands can be applied to images, and also individual layers in layered images. This can be useful for positioning items and also for correcting the orientation of an image that is on its side or upside down.

Rotating a whole image

 Select **Image > Rotate** from the Menu bar

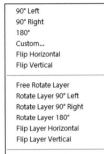

90° Left
90° Right
180°
Custom...
Flip Horizontal
Flip Vertical
Free Rotate Layer
Rotate Layer 90° Left
Rotate Layer 90° Right
Rotate Layer 180°
Flip Layer Horizontal
Flip Layer Vertical
Straighten and Crop Image
Straighten Image

Select a rotation option from the menu

Select **Custom** to enter your own value for the amount you want an image rotated

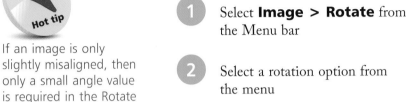

Click on the **OK** button

Rotating a layer
To rotate separate layers within an image:

Open an image that consists of two or more layers. Select one of the layers in the Layers panel

Select **Image > Rotate** from the Menu bar

Select a layer rotation option from the menu

The selected layer is rotated independently

Transforming

The Transform commands can be used to resize an image, and to apply some basic distortion techniques. These commands can be accessed by selecting **Image > Transform** from the Menu bar.

Free Transform

This enables you to manually alter the size and shape of an image. To do this:

 1   Select **Image > Transform > Free Transform** from the Menu bar

2   Click and drag here to transform the vertical and horizontal size of the image. Hold down **Shift** to transform it in proportion

The other options from the Transform menu are Skew, Distort and Perspective. These can be accessed and applied in a similar way to the Free Transform option.

Magnification

There are a number of ways in Elements in which the magnification at which an image is being viewed can be increased or decreased. This can be useful if you want to zoom in on a particular part of an image, for editing purposes, or if you want to view a whole image to see the result of editing effects that have been applied.

View menu

The View menu can be used to display rulers at the top and left of an image, which can be useful for precise measurement and placement. There is also a command for displaying a grid over the top of the whole image.

 Select **View** from the Menu bar and select one of the options from the View menu

View	Window	Help
New Window for bulgaria4.jpg		
Zoom In		Ctrl+=
Zoom Out		Ctrl+-
Fit on Screen		Ctrl+0
Actual Pixels		Ctrl+1
Print Size		
Selection		Ctrl+H
Rulers		Shift+Ctrl+R
Grid		Ctrl+'

Zoom tool

① Select the **Zoom** tool from the Toolbox

② Click once on an image to enlarge it (usually by 100% each time). Hold down **Alt** and click to decrease the magnification

Click and drag with the Zoom tool over a small area to increase the magnification to the maximum, i.e. 3200%. This can be particularly useful when performing close-up editing tasks, such as removing red-eye.

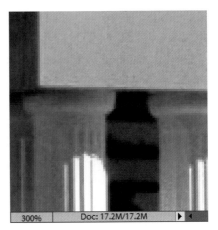

Navigator panel

This can be used to move around an image and also magnify certain areas. To use the Navigator panel:

 Access the **Navigator** panel by selecting **Window > Navigator** from the Menu bar

Drag this slider to magnify the area of the image within the red rectangle

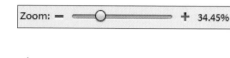

The Navigator also has buttons for zooming in and out. These are located at the left and right of the slider.

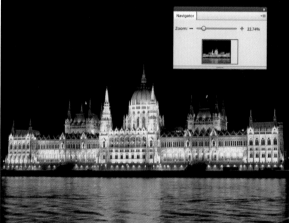

Drag the rectangle to change the area of the image that is being magnified

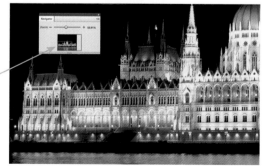

Eraser

The Eraser tool can be used to remove areas of an image. In a simple, single layer image, this can just leave a blank hole, which has to be filled with something. The Eraser options are:

The Background Eraser tool can be used to remove an uneven background. To do this, drag over the background with the Background Eraser tool and, depending on the settings in the Tool Options panel, everything that it is dragged over will be removed.

1 **Eraser**, which can be used to erase part of the background image or a layer within it

2 **Background Eraser**, which can be used to remove an uneven background

3 **Magic Eraser**, which can be used to quickly remove a solid background (see below)

Erasing a background

With the Magic Eraser tool, it is possible to delete a colored background in an image. To do this:

1 Open an image with an evenly-colored background

2 Select the **Magic Eraser** and make the required selections in the Tool Options panel. Make sure the Contiguous box is not checked

3 Click once on the background. It is removed from the image, regardless of where it occurs

If the **Contiguous** box is not checked, the background color will be removed wherever it occurs in the image. If the Contiguous box is checked, the background color will only be removed where it touches another area of the same color, which is not broken by another element of the image.

4 Quick Wins

This chapter looks at some of the "quick wins" that can be done in Elements, such as removing unwanted objects and changing photos to black and white. It also shows some of the Guided and Quick edit options that provide step-by-step actions for creating a range of creative and striking photos.

70 Removing Red-eye

72 Quickly Removing Items

74 Content-Aware Editing

76 Changing to Black and White

78 Quick Edit Mode Options

79 Quick Edit Toolbox

80 Quick Edit Adjustments

82 Enhancing with Quick Edits

84 Using Guided Edit Mode

86 Photomerge Effects

88 Photomerge Compose

90 Panoramas

Removing Red-eye

One of the most common problems with photographs of people, whether they are taken digitally or with a film-based camera, is red-eye. This is caused when the camera's flash is used and then reflects in the subject's pupils. This can create the dreaded red-eye effect, when the subject can unintentionally be transformed into a demonic character.

Elements has recognized that removing red-eye is one of the top priorities for most amateur photographers and a specific tool for this purpose has been included in the Toolbox: the Red Eye Removal tool. This is available in Expert or Quick edit modes:

 Open an image that contains red-eye

 Select the **Zoom** tool from the Toolbox

 Drag around the affected area until it appears at a suitable magnification. Select the **Red Eye Removal** tool from the Toolbox

 Click in the Tool Options panel to select the size of the pupil and the amount by which it will be darkened

⑤ Click once on the red-eye, or drag around the affected area to remove the red-eye

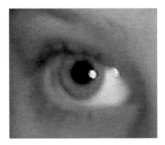

Hot tip

The best way to deal with red-eye is to avoid it in the first place. Try using a camera that has a red-eye reduction function. This uses an extra flash, just before the picture is taken, to diminish the effect of red-eye.

Hot tip

In Guided edit mode, the Perfect Portrait option (in the Touchups section) also has a red-eye removal function.

Hot tip

Red-eye can be removed automatically by clicking on the **Auto Correct** button in the Red Eye Removal Tool Options panel.

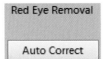

Pet Red-eye removal

Photos of animals and pets are another popular area for photographers but these can suffer from red-eye (or other color distortions) in the same way as for people. To overcome this there is also a pet red-eye removal tools. To use this:

 Open an image of a pet or an animal that contains red-eye

 Select the **Red Eye Removal** tool from the Toolbox

 Check on the **Pet Eye** box in the Tool Options

Red Eye Removal

Auto Correct

☑ Pet Eye

 Use the Zoom tool as in Step 2 on the previous page and zoom in on the affected area

Hot tip

Red-eye can also be removed when images are being downloaded from the camera. This is an option in the Photo Downloader window.

 Click on the affected area to remove the red-eye

Quickly Removing Items

One of the most annoying aspects of taking photos is to capture what you think is a perfect image, only to find that there is an unwanted object in the final shot. In Elements it is possible to delete unwanted items and automatically fill-in the area from where these are removed. To do this:

 Open an image which contains an unwanted object

Hot tip

The selection around the object does not have to be too accurate, as long as it goes around the border of the object.

 Use one of the selection tools to select the unwanted object

Lasso

 Select **Edit > Fill Selection** from the Menu bar

Edit	Image	Enhance	Layer
Undo Lasso			Ctrl+Z
Redo Fill			Ctrl+Y
Revert			Shift+Ctrl+A
Cut			Ctrl+X
Copy			Ctrl+C
Copy Merged			Shift+Ctrl+C
Paste			Ctrl+V
Paste Into Selection			Shift+Ctrl+V
Delete			
Fill Selection...			

4 Make the selections in the Fill Layer dialog box. Ensure **Content-Aware** is selected in the **Contents** section

Fill Layer ✕

⊘ Learn more about: Fill Layer

OK

Cancel

Contents
Use: Content-Aware ▾

Custom Pattern: ▾

Blending
Mode: Normal ▾

Opacity: 100 %

☐ Preserve Transparency

5 Click on the **OK** button

6 The selection is deleted and the area is automatically filled with the background

Beware

If there are too many colors around the selected area the fill effect may appear inaccurate. If this is the case, try with a slightly different selection area.

7 The final image makes it appear that the unwanted object was never there in the first place

Content-Aware Editing

Unless you are taking photos under studio conditions it is probable that you will get some unwanted items in your photos, or the composition may not be exactly as you would like it in terms of the position of the subjects. The answer to this is the Content-Aware editing tool. This can be used to move subjects in a photo and then have the background behind them filled in automatically.

1 Open an image with a subject that you want to move

2 Select the **Content-Aware Move** tool from the Toolbox

3 Check on the **Move** box in Tool Options

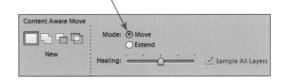

4 Drag around the subject that you want to move

5 Drag the subject to a new position

6 The area where the subject was previously located is filled in by the Content-Aware function

Don't forget

The Content-Aware tool can also be used to extend areas within an image. To do this, check on the **Extend** box in Tool Options, drag around the area you want to extend and the drag the selection into place. The Content-Aware Move tool will automatically fill in the background for the area that is extended.

Changing to Black and White

Most digital cameras and scanners are capable of converting color images into black and white at the point of capture. However, it is also possible to use Elements to convert existing color images into black and white ones. To do this:

When creating black and white images, make a copy of the original first. Use the copy to create the new image.

1 Open a color image and select **Enhance > Convert to Black and White** from the Menu bar

2 The Convert to Black and White dialog box has various options for how the image is converted

3 Select the type of black and white effect to be applied, depending on the subject in the image

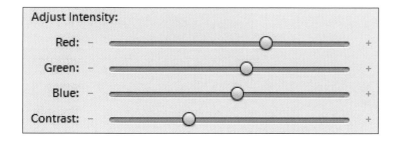

Select a style:

Infrared Effect
Newspaper
Portraits
Scenic Landscape
Urban/Snapshots
Vivid Landscapes

4 Drag these sliders to specify the intensity of the effect to be applied for different elements

Adjust Intensity:

Red: – +
Green: – +
Blue: – +
Contrast: – +

5 Click on the **OK** button

OK

6 The image is converted into black and white, according to the settings that have been selected

Hot tip

A similar effect can be achieved by selecting **Enhance > Adjust Color > Remove Color** from the Menu bar.

Quick Edit Mode Options

The Quick edit options in Elements offer a number of functions within the one location. This makes it easier to apply a number of techniques at the same time.

Using Quick edit mode

 Open an image in the Editor and click on the **Quick** button

 The Quick edit mode has a modified Toolbox, with fewer tools, that is displayed here

Hot tip

The Exposure panel is a good option for quickly editing photos that are under- or over-exposed, i.e. too dark or too light.

 Click on bottom toolbar to access the Quick Edit panel options. The default one is for **Adjustments**

 Click on the **Adjustments** panels to make the appropriate changes (see pages 80-81)

78

Quick Edit Toolbox

The Quick Edit Toolbox has a reduced Toolbox that includes:

- Zoom tool
- Hand tool
- Quick Selection tool
- Red-eye Removal tool
- Whiten Teeth tool
- Text tool
- Spot Healing/Healing tool
- Crop tool
- Move tool

Whitening teeth

One of the tool options in the Quick edit mode Toolbox is for whitening teeth in a photo. To do this:

1 Open an image and click on the **Whiten Teeth** tool and select a brush size for the Whiten Teeth tool

2 Drag the Whiten Teeth tool over the teeth

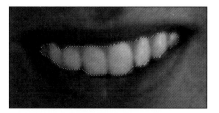

3 The teeth area is selected and whitened in one operation

Quick Edit Adjustments

The adjustment panels in the Quick edit section are:

Smart Fix panel

This performs several editing changes in a single operation. Click on the Auto button to have the changes applied automatically, or drag the slider to specify the amount of the editing changes. Click on the thumbnails to apply preset amounts of the change.

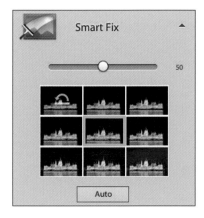

Changes are displayed in the main Quick edit window as they are being made.

Exposure panel

This provides options for adjusting the lighting and contrast in an image. Drag the sliders to adjust the exposure or click on one of the thumbnails to apply a preset option.

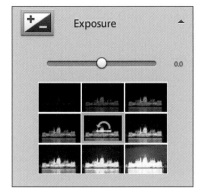

Lighting panel

This provides options for adjusting the lightest and darkest points in an image. This is done by adjusting the shadows, midtones and highlights in an image. Drag the slider to adjust this or click on one of the thumbnails for an auto option.

Color panel

Click on the Auto button to adjust the hue and saturation in an image, or drag the slider to make manual adjustments. Click on the thumbnails to apply preset amounts.

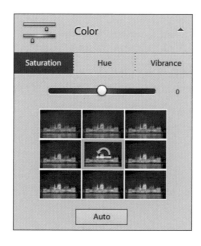

The Balance panel can be used to create some abstract color effects.

Balance panel

Drag the slider to adjust the warmth of the colors in an image and the color balance. Click on the thumbnails to apply preset amounts.

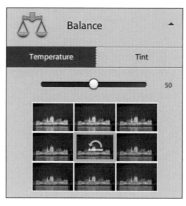

Sharpening works by increasing the contrast between adjoining pixels to make the overall image appear more in focus. It can also be accessed by selecting **Enhance > Auto Sharpen** or **Enhance > Unsharp Mask** from the Expert menu bar. The Unsharp Mask option has a dialog window where the effect can be added as a percentage.

Sharpen panel

This can be used to apply sharpening to an image to make it clearer, either automatically with the Auto button, or the panel thumbnails, or manually with the slider.

Enhancing with Quick Edits

In addition to the Adjustments option, the other buttons on the Quick edit toolbar are for adding Effects, Textures and Frames to your photos. They can be used individually, or in combination, to enhance your photos so that they will really stand out for your family and friends. To begin, open the image which you want to enhance with the Quick edit options:

Effects

To add photo effects to your images:

The Effects panel has been updated in Elements 13 and, in Quick edit mode, there are now sub-categories for the main categories, i.e. the Seasons category has Summer, Autumn, Winter and Snow. Move the cursor over a category and click on the down-pointing arrow to view the sub-categories.

 1 Click on the **Effects** button on the Quick Edit toolbar

 2 Click on one of the Effects options to apply that to the currently active image

Textures

To add texture effects to your images:

 Click on the **Textures** button on the Quick Edit editing panel

 Click on one of the Textures options to apply that to the currently active image

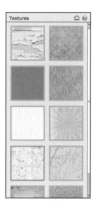

Frames

To add frame effects to your images:

 Click on the **Frames** button on the Quick Edit toolbar

 Click on one of the Frames options to apply that to the currently active image

The effects are added to the image:

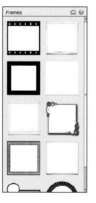

Hot tip

Save the file in a .PSD or .PDD format (a proprietary Photoshop format) to preserve the items added in Quick edit mode, so that they can be edited again when the file is opened. Save it in a JPEG format to merge all of the layers, in which case they will not be able to be edited separately.

Using Guided Edit Mode

In Elements, the Guided edit function has been enhanced to make it easier to perform both simple editing functions and also more complex image-editing processes that consist of a number of steps. To use the various functions of Guided edit mode:

 1 Open an image and click on the **Guided** button

Guided

2 In the **Touchups** section, select a function such as Brightness and Contrast

Touchups ⌃

Brightness and Contrast

Correct Skin Tones

Crop Photo

Enhance Colors

Levels

3 Details of the selected function are displayed. Click on the **Auto Fix** button or drag the sliders to apply the effects for the selected function

Brightness and Contrast ↺ ❓

Auto Fix

Click Auto Fix to apply a general fix to under- or over-exposed images.

Brightness: ⎯⎯⎯⎯⎯○⎯⎯⎯⎯

Contrast: ⎯⎯⎯⎯○⎯⎯⎯⎯⎯

Drag these sliders to fine-tune the difference between pure black and pure white.

 4 Click on the **Done** button

 Done

Photo Effects and Photo Play

In addition to one-step Guided edits there are also more in-depth operations such as Photo Effects and Photo Play. These contain a number of editing techniques, which you are taken through in a step-by-step process to create the final effect:

1 Click on one of the options under **Photo Effects** or **Photo Play**. The Photo Effects include items such as creating depth of field effects, color effects such as high key, to give a photo a surreal brightness, and traditional photography effects such as the Lomo Camera Effect and the Orton Effect. The Photo Play effects are for special effects such as making one element appear out of the rest of the photo, a broken up Picture Stack, Pop Art effect and a Reflection of the selected image

For details of some of the Photo Effects and Photo Play effects, see pages 158-166.

2 Click on each of the buttons to apply the required effects. Some of these have additional dialog boxes where settings for the effect can be applied

3 If you do not like the appearance of the photo, click on the **Reset** button to return to its original state

4 Click on the **Done** button to complete the Guided edit

Photomerge Effects

Within Elements there are a number of Photomerge effects that can be used to combine elements from different photos to create a new image. This can be used to remove items from photos, combine elements from two, or more, photos and match the exposure from different photos.

To access the Photomerge options, select **Enhance > Photomerge** from within any of the Editor modes.

| Photomerge® Compose... |
| Photomerge® Exposure... |
| Photomerge® Faces... |
| Photomerge® Group Shot... |
| Photomerge® Panorama... |
| Photomerge® Scene Cleaner... |

Don't forget

The Pencil tool is used for several of the Photomerge options. It is used to draw over an area in a source image that is then merged into the final image.

The Photomerge options are:

- **Compose.** This can be used to merge a part of one image with the background of another, see pages 88-89.

- **Exposure.** This can be used to create a well-exposed photo from a series of photos of the same shot that have different exposures, i.e. one may be over-exposed and another under-exposed. The Photomerge effect combines the photos so that the final one is correctly exposed. This can be done with the **Automatic** option, or the **Manual** one.

Beware

For the Exposure Photomerge function, all of the photos used have to be of exactly the same shot, otherwise there will be some overlap in the final image.

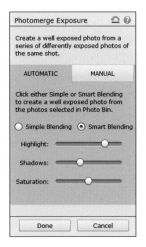

- **Faces.** This is an option for combining features of two faces together. This is done by opening photos of two people and then aligning the features of one so that they are merged with the other.

- **Group Shot.** This can be used to add or delete people from group shots. This is done by opening two, or more, photos of the group. Use the **Pencil** tool to merge a person from one photo into the other and the **Eraser** tool to delete any areas that you do not want copied to the new photo.

- **Panorama.** This can be used to create panoramas with two, or more, photos (see pages 90-92 for details).

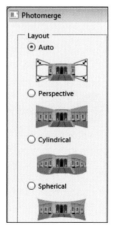

- **Scene Cleaner.** This can be used to remove unwanted elements in a photo. This is done by using two, or more, similar photos, with elements that you want to remove, then merging the elements that you want to keep into the final photo.

Photomerge Compose

One of the Photomerge effects, which is new in Elements 13, is the Compose option. This can be used to combine a selection from one photo with the background of another. This can be used for a variety of subjects, from landscape, to adding people to group shots when they were not there at the time. To do this:

 Open the two photos that you want to use, in the Editor, or select them in the Organizer

 Select **Edit > Photomerge > Photomerge Compose** from the Menu bar

Click on the **Advanced Edge Refinement** button to access options for how the edges of the selection appear.

 For the image from which you want to make a selection, drag it into the main window

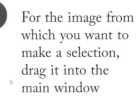

 Select one of the tools for making the selection

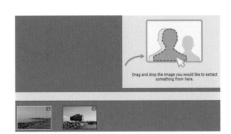

Trace around the area
you want to select. The
rest of the image will
have a red mask placed
over it. Click on the
Next button

 Click on the **Move and Resize tool**
button to move, or resize, the selection
on the background image

Click on the **Hide** or **Reveal** buttons
to draw over areas of the selection that
you want removed, or areas below that
you want to be visible. Click on the
Next button

Click on the **Auto Match Color
Tone** button to blend the selection area
with the background. Drag the sliders to
make alterations manually

Click on the **Done** button

The selection can be
resized by dragging
the resizing handles
that appear around
its border. Hold down
the Shift key at the
same time to resize the
selection proportionally.

The selection
is merged
with the
background

Panoramas

Creating panoramas

For anyone who takes landscape pictures, the desire to create a panorama occurs sooner or later. With film-based cameras, this usually involves sticking several photographs together to create the panorama, albeit a rather patchwork one. With digital images the end result can look a lot more professional and Elements has a dedicated function for achieving this: the Photomerge Panorama.

When creating a panorama there are a few rules to follow:

● If possible, use a tripod to ensure that your camera stays at the same level for all of the shots.

● Keep the same exposure settings for all images.

● Make sure that there is a reasonable overlap between images (about 20%). Some cameras enable you to align the correct overlap between the images.

● Keep the same distance between yourself and the object you are capturing. Otherwise the end result will look out of perspective.

To create a panorama:

 In Expert edit mode open two or more images and select **Enhance > Photomerge > Photomerge Panorama** from the Menu bar

 Select an option for the type of panorama image that you want to create

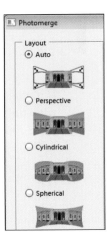

 Beware

Do not include too many images in a panorama, otherwise it could be too large for viewing or printing easily.

3 Click on the **Browse** button to locate images you want to use on your computer

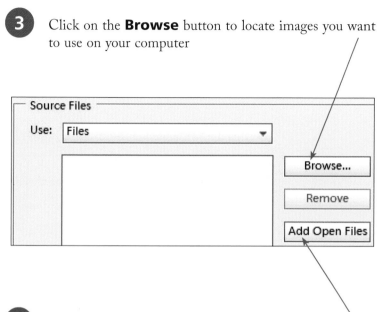

4 Or click on the **Add Open Files** button to use images that are already open

5 If you Browse for images, select them from your computer

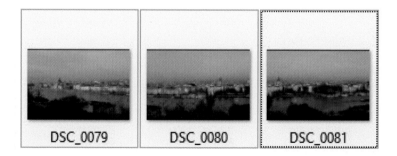

DSC_0079   DSC_0080   DSC_0081

6 Click on the **OK** button

OK

Hot tip

Panoramas do not just have to be of landscapes. They can also be used for items, such as a row of buildings or crowds at a sporting event.

...cont'd

 The panorama will be created, but with gaps where the images could not be matched. The **Clean Edges** dialog box asks if you would like to fill in the edges of the panorama. Click on the **Yes** button to blend the empty areas with the background

 Panoramas can usually be improved by applying color correction such as Brightness/Contrast and Shadows/Highlights. They can also be cropped to make a narrower panorama to highlight the main subject

5 Beyond the Basics

This chapter looks at some of the more powerful features for image editing in Elements, so you can take your skills to the next level.

94 Hue and Saturation

96 Histogram

98 Levels

100 Importing RAW Images

102 Image Size

104 Resampling Images

Hue and Saturation

The hue and saturation command can be used to edit the color elements of an image. However, it works slightly differently from other commands, such as those for the brightness and contrast. There are three areas that are covered by the hue and saturation command: color, color strength and lightness. To adjust the hue and saturation of an image:

 Open an image

 Select **Enhance > Adjust Color > Adjust Hue/ Saturation** from the Menu bar, in either Expert or Quick edit modes

Hot tip

By altering the hue of an image, some interesting abstract color effects can be created. This can be very effective if you are producing several versions of the same image, such as for an artistic poster.

Don't forget

Hue is used to describe the color of a particular pixel or an image.

Drag this slider to adjust the hue of the image, i.e. change the colors in the image

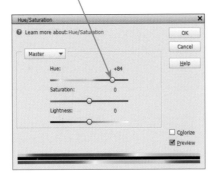

4 Drag this slider to adjust the saturation, i.e. the intensity of colors in the image

The Lightness option is similar to adjusting image brightness.

5 Check on the **Colorize** box to color the image with the hue of the currently-selected foreground color in the Color Picker, which is located at the bottom of the Toolbox

The Colorize option can be used to create some interesting "color wash" effects. Try altering the Hue slider once the Colorize box has been checked on.

6 Click on the **OK** button to apply any changes that have been made

For more on working with color and the Color Picker, see pages 147-148.

Histogram

The histogram is a device that displays the tonal range of the pixels in an image, and it can be used for very precise editing of an image. The histogram (**Window > Histogram** in Expert edit mode) is a graph which displays how the pixels in an image are distributed across the image, from the darkest (black) to the lightest (white) points. Another way of considering the histogram is that it displays the values of an image's highlights, midtones and shadows:

Don't forget

The histogram works by looking at the individual color channels of an image (Red, Green, Blue, also known as the RGB color model) or at a combination of all three, which is displayed as the Luminosity in the Channel box. It can also look at all of the colors in an image.

Don't forget

Image formats, such as JPEG, are edited in Elements using the RGB color model, i.e. red, green and blue mixed together to create the colors in the image.

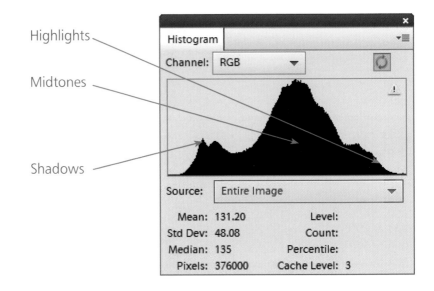

...cont'd

Ideally, the histogram should show a reasonably consistent range of tonal distribution, indicating an image that has good contrast and detail:

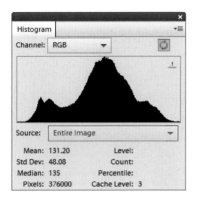

However, if the tonal range is bunched at one end of the graph, this indicates that the image is under-exposed or over-exposed:

Over-exposure

Under-exposure

Hot tip

If the histogram is left open, it will update automatically as editing changes are made to an image. This gives a good idea of how effective the changes are.

Levels

While the histogram displays the tonal range of an image, the Levels function can be used to edit this range. Any changes made using the Levels function will then be visible in the histogram. Levels allow you to redistribute pixels between the darkest and lightest points in an image, and also to set these points manually if you want to. To use the Levels function:

Hot tip

The Levels function can be used to adjust the tonal range of a specific area of an image, by first making a selection and then using the Levels dialog box. For more details on selecting areas see Chapter Six.

Don't forget

In the Levels dialog box, the graph is the same as the one shown in the histogram.

Don't forget

Image shadows, midtones and highlights can be altered by dragging the markers for the black, midtone and white input points.

1 Open an image

2 Select **Enhance > Adjust Lighting > Levels** from the Menu bar, in either Expert or Quick edit modes

Midtone input point

Black input point

White input point

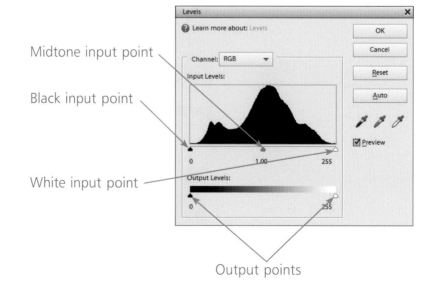

Output points

3 Drag the black point and the white point sliders to, or beyond, the first pixels denoted in the graph to increase the contrast

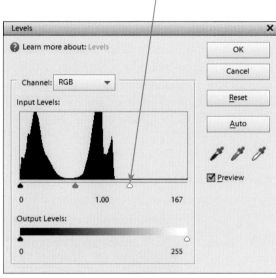

66

4 Drag the output sliders towards the middle to decrease the contrast

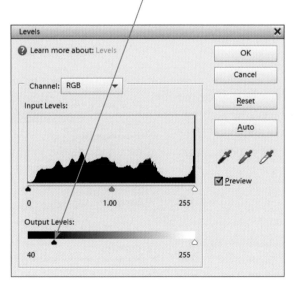

Importing RAW Images

RAW images are those in which the digital data has not been processed in any way, or converted into any specific file format, by the camera when they were captured. These produce high quality images and are usually available on higher specification digital cameras. However, RAW is becoming more common in consumer digital cameras and they can be downloaded in Elements in the same way as any other image. Once the RAW images are accessed, the Camera Raw dialog box opens so that a variety of editing functions can be applied to the image. RAW images act as a digital negative and have to be saved into another format before they can be used in the conventional way. To edit RAW images:

Beware

RAW images are much larger in file size than the same versions captured as JPEGs.

 Open a RAW image in the Editor or from the Organizer

In the Camera RAW dialog box, editing functions that are usually performed when an image is captured can be made manually

Hot tip

All images can be open in RAW by using the **File > Open in Camera Raw** command from the Menu bar.

Click here to adjust the White Balance in the image

White Balance:	As Shot
Temperature	As Shot
	Auto
	Daylight
Tint	Cloudy
	Shade
	Tungsten
	Fluorescent
	Flash
Exposure	Custom

 Drag these sliders to adjust the Color Temperature and Tint in the image

| Temperature | 4850 |
| Tint | +12 |

Drag these sliders to adjust the Exposure, Shadows, Brightness, Contrast and Saturation in the image

	Auto	Default
Exposure		0.00
Contrast		0
Highlights		0
Shadows		0
Whites		0
Blacks		0

 Click on the **Detail** tab and drag these sliders to adjust the Sharpness and Noise in the image

Detail

Sharpening

Amount	25
Radius	1.0
Detail	25
Masking	0

Noise Reduction

Luminance	0
Luminance Detail	
Luminance Contrast	
Color	25

 Click on the **Open Image** button. This opens the image in Expert edit mode, from where it can also be saved as a standard file format, such as JPEG

Don't forget

The RAW format should be used if you want to make manual changes to an image to achieve the highest possible quality.

Image Size

The physical size of a digital image can sometimes be a confusing issue, as it is frequently dealt with under the term "resolution". Unfortunately, resolution can be applied to a number of areas of digital imaging: image resolution, monitor resolution, print size and print resolution.

Image resolution

The resolution of an image is determined by the number of pixels in it. This is counted as a vertical and a horizontal value, e.g. 4000 x 3000. When multiplied together it gives the overall resolution, i.e. 12,000,000 pixels in this case. This is frequently the headline figure quoted by the manufacturers, e.g. 12 million pixels (or 12 megapixels). To view the image resolution in Elements:

Hot tip

To view an image at its actual size, or the size at which it will currently be printed, select the **Zoom** tool from the Toolbox and select **1:1** or **Print Size** from the Tool Options panel.

1 Select **Image > Resize > Image Size** from the Menu bar

2 The image size is displayed here (in pixels)

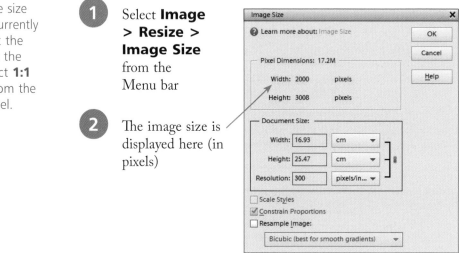

Don't forget

The Resolution figure under the Document Size heading is used to determine the size at which the image will be printed. If this is set to 72 pixels/inch, then the onscreen size and the printed size should be roughly the same.

Monitor resolution

Most modern computer monitors display digital images at between 72 and 96 pixels per inch (PPI). This means that every inch of the screen contains approximately this number of pixels. So, for an image being displayed at 100%, the onscreen size will be the number of pixels horizontally divided by 72 (or 96 depending on the monitor) and the same vertically. In the above example, this would mean the image would be viewed at 34 inches by 45 inches approximately (2448/72 and 3264/72) on a monitor. In modern web browsers this is usually adjusted so that the whole image is accommodated on the viewable screen.

Document size (print resolution)

Pixels in an image are not a set size, which means that images can be printed in a variety of sizes, simply by contracting or expanding the available pixels. This is done by changing the resolution in the Document Size section of the Image Size dialog box. (When dealing with document size, think of this as the size of the printed document.) To set the size at which an image will be printed:

Hot tip

To work out the size at which an image will be printed, divide the pixel dimensions (height and width) by the resolution value under the Document Size heading.

 1 Select **Image > Resize > Image Size** from the Menu bar

2 Change the resolution here (or change the Width and Height of the document size). Make sure the Resample Image box is not checked

Image Size

Learn more about: Image Size

Pixel Dimensions: 17.2M

Width: 2000 pixels
Height: 3008 pixels

Document Size:

Width: 33.87 cm
Height: 50.94 cm
Resolution: 150 pixels/in...

☐ Scale Styles
☑ Constrain Proportions
☐ Resample Image:
Bicubic (best for smooth gradients)

OK / Cancel / Help

Don't forget

The print resolution determines how many pixels are used in each inch of the printed image (PPI). However, the number of dots used to represent each pixel on the paper is determined by the printer resolution, measured in dots per inch (DPI). So if the print resolution is 72 PPI and the printer resolution is 2880 DPI, each pixel will be represented by 40 colored dots, i.e. 2880 divided by 72.

3 By changing one value, the other two are updated too. Click on the **OK** button

Document Size:

Width: 20 cm
Height: 30.08 cm
Resolution: 254 pixels/in...

 OK

Resampling Images

All digital images can be increased or decreased in size. This involves adding or removing pixels from the image. Decreasing the size of an image is relatively straightforward and involves removing redundant pixels. However, increasing the size of an image involves adding pixels by digital guesswork. To do this, Elements looks at the existing pixels and works out the nearest match for the ones that are to be added. Increasing or decreasing the size of a digital image is known as "resampling".

Resampling

Resampling down decreases the size of the image and it is more effective than resampling up. To do this:

104

1 Select **Image > Resize > Image Size** from the Menu bar

2 Check on the **Resample Image** box

3 Resample the image by changing the pixel dimensions, the height and width or the resolution

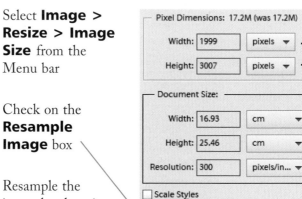

4 Changing any of the values above alters the physical size of the image. Click on the **OK** button

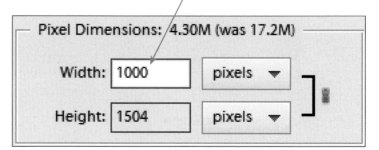

6 Selecting Areas

The true power of digital image editing comes into its own when you are able to select areas of an image and edit them independently. This chapter looks at the various ways that selections can be made and edited, using the tools and functions within Elements.

106   About Selections

107   Marquee Tools

108   Lasso Tools

110   Magic Wand Tool

111   Selection Brush Tool

112   Quick Selection Tool

113   Smart Brush Tool

114   Inverting a Selection

115   Feathering

116   Refining Selections

118   Editing Selections

Don't forget

Once a selection has been made it stays selected, even when another tool is activated, to allow for editing to take place.

Hot tip

The best way to deselect a selection is to click on it once with one of the selection tools, preferably the one used to make the selection.

About Selections

One of the most important aspects of image editing is the ability to select areas within an image. This can be used in a number of different ways:

- Selecting an object to apply an editing technique to it (such as changing the brightness or contrast) without affecting the rest of the image

- Selecting a particular color in an image

- Selecting an area on which to apply a special effect

- Selecting an area to remove

Expert edit mode has several tools that can be used to select items, and there are also a number of editing functions that can be applied to selections.

Two examples of how selections can be used are:

 Select an area within an image and delete it

 Select an area and add a color or special effect

Marquee Tools

There are two options for the Marquee tool: the Rectangular Marquee tool and the Elliptical Marquee tool. Both of these can be used to make symmetrical selections. To use the Marquee tools:

1 Select either the **Rectangular** or the **Elliptical Marquee** tool from the Toolbox. Select the required options from the Tool Options panel

2 Make a symmetrical selection with one of the tools by clicking and dragging on an image

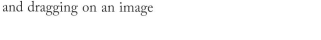

Elliptical selection   Rectangular selection

To access additional tools from the Expert edit mode Toolbox, click on a tool and select any grouped tools in the Tool Options panel.

To make a selection that is exactly square or round, hold down Shift when dragging with the Rectangular Marquee tool or the Elliptical Marquee tool respectively.

Lasso Tools

There are three options for the Lasso tools, which can be used to make freehand selections. To use these:

Lasso tool

 Select the **Lasso** tool from the Toolbox and select the required options from the Tool Options panel

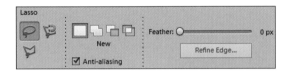

 Make a freehand selection by clicking and dragging around an object

Polygonal Lasso tool

 Select the **Polygonal Lasso** tool from the Toolbox and select the required options from the Tool Options panel

 Make a selection by clicking on specific points around an object, and then dragging to the next point

Making a selection with the Polygonal Lasso tool is like creating a dot-to-dot pattern.

Magnetic Lasso tool

 Select the **Magnetic Lasso** tool from the Toolbox and select the required options from the Tool Options panel

 Click once on an image to create the first anchor point

 Make a selection by dragging continuously around an object. The selection line snaps to the closest, strongest edge, i.e. the one with the most contrast. Fastening points are added as the selection is made

Magic Wand Tool

The Magic Wand tool can be used to select areas of the same, or similar, color. To do this:

In the Tool Options panel for the Magic Wand tool, the Tolerance box determines the range of colors that will be selected in relation to the color you click on. A low value will only select a very narrow range of colors in relation to the initially-selected one, while a high value will include a greater range. The values range from 0-255.

In the Tool Options panel for the Magic Wand tool, check on the **Contiguous** box to ensure that only adjacent colors are selected. To select the same, or similar, color throughout the image, whether adjacent or not, uncheck the Contiguous box.

 Select the **Magic Wand** tool from the Toolbox and select the required options from the Tool Options panel

 Click on a color to select all of the adjacent pixels that are the same or similar color, depending on the options selected from the Tool Options panel

Selection Brush Tool

The Selection Brush tool can be used to select areas by using a brush-like stroke. Unlike with the Marquee or Lasso tools, the area selected by the Selection Brush tool is the one directly below where the tool moves. To make a selection with the Selection Brush tool (this is also available in Quick edit mode):

 Select the **Selection Brush** tool from the Toolbox and select the required options from the Tool Options panel

The Selection Brush tool can be used to select an area, or to mask an area. This can be determined in the Selection box in the Tool Options panel.

2 Click and drag to make a selection

3 The selection area is underneath the borders of the Selection Brush tool

Quick Selection Tool

The Quick Selection tool can be used to select areas of similar color by drawing over the general area, without having to make a specific selection. To do this:

 Select the **Quick Selection** tool from the Toolbox

 Select the required options from the Tool Options panel

The Quick Selection tool is also available from the Quick edit mode Toolbox.

 Draw over an area, or part of an area, to select all of the similarly-colored pixels

Smart Brush Tool

The Smart Brush tool can be used to quickly select large areas in an image (in a similar way to the Quick Selection tool) and then have effects applied automatically to the selected area. To do this:

 Open the image to which you want to apply changes

 Select the **Smart Brush** tool from the Toolbox

 Select the editing effect you want to apply to the area selected by the Smart Brush tool, from the Tool Options panel

4 Select **Brush size** for the Smart Brush tool, from the Tool Options panel

5 Drag the Smart Brush tool over an area of the image. In the left-hand image below, the building has been selected and brightened; in the right-hand image the sky has been selected and enhanced

Inverting a Selection

This can be a useful option if you have edited a selection and then want to edit the rest of the image without affecting the area you have just selected. To do this:

 Make a selection

Hot tip

When inverting a selection, ensure that the whole of the required area has been selected. If not, hold down **Shift** and make another selection to add this to the existing one.

 Choose **Select > Inverse** from the Menu bar

 The selection becomes inverted, i.e. if a background object was selected the foreground is now selected

Feathering

Feathering is a technique that can be used to soften the edges of a selection by making them slightly blurry. This can be used if you are pasting a selection into another image, or if you want to soften the edges around a portrait of an individual. To do this:

 Make a selection

2 Choose **Select > Feather** from the Menu bar

Feathering can also be selected from the Tool Options panel once a Marquee tool is selected, and before the selection has been made.

3 Enter a Feather value (the number of pixels around the radius of the selection

that will be blurred). Click on the **OK** button

If required, crop the final image so that the feathered subject is more prominent.

4 Invert the selection, as shown on the previous page, and delete the background by pressing **Delete** on the keyboard. This will leave the selection around the subject with softened edges

Refining Selections

When making selections it is sometimes difficult to exactly select the area that you want. In Elements 13 it is now possible to refine the area of a selection and also the edges around a selected item.

The **Refine Selection Brush** option can be used regardless of how the selection was made.

1 In Expert or Quick mode, make a selection with one of the selection tools

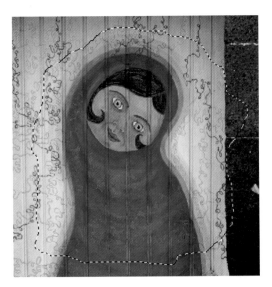

2 Select the **Refine Selection Brush** tool (grouped with the Quick Selection tool)

3 Click on this button to select to manipulate the selection with the cursor

4 Click on this button to smooth the edges of the selection by dragging the cursor over it

5 Select a size for the cursor for refining the selection and the strength for how it snaps to neighboring pixels; the greater the strength the more the selection will snap to pixels of similar color

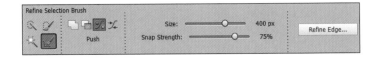

6 Position the cursor inside or outside the selection. It appears as two circles, a smaller one inside a larger one. Use the circles to nudge the selection lines one way or another to refine the selection

Refining edges

It is also possible to add a range of refinements to the edges of a selection, which can be an excellent option for textures such as clothing or animal fur. To do this:

1 Once a selection has been made, click on the **Refine Edge** button in the selections Tool Options panel

Refine Edge...

2 Select options here for how much of the edge is detected in terms of being refined. Select **Smart Radius** or enter a manual value for the radius

Hot tip

The Refine Edge options are particularly useful if you are copying a selection and pasting it into another image, that has different textures.

3 Select options here for how the edge is adjusted, using smoothing, feathering, contrast and moving the edge. Click **OK**

Editing Selections

When you have made a selection, you can edit it in a number of ways:

Moving a selection
Make a selection and select the **Move** tool from the Toolbox. Drag the selection to move it to a new location.

Changing the selection area
Make a selection with a selection tool. With the same tool selected, click and drag within the selection area to move it over another part of the image.

Adding to a selection
Make a selection and click on this button in the Tool Options panel. Make another selection to create a single larger selection. The two selections do not have to intersect.

Intersecting with a selection
To create a selection by intersecting two existing selections: make a selection and click on this button in the Tool Options panel. Make another selection that intersects the first. The intersected area will become the selection.

Expanding a selection
To expand a selection by a specific number of pixels: make a selection and choose **Select > Modify > Expand** from the Menu bar. In the **Expand Selection** dialog box, enter the amount by which you want the selection expanded.

Growing a selection
The Grow command can be used on a selection when it has been made with the Magic Wand tool, and some of the pixels within the selection have been omitted. To do this:

 Make a selection with the **Magic Wand** tool and make the required choices from the Tool Options panel

 Choose **Select > Grow** from the Menu bar

Depending on the choices in the Tool Options panel, the omitted pixels will be included in the selection.

Beware

Once an area has been moved and deselected, it cannot then be selected independently again, unless it has been copied and pasted onto a separate layer.

Don't forget

To deselect a selection, click once inside the selection area with the tool that was used to make the selection.

7 Layers

Layers provide the means to add numerous elements to an image, and edit them independently from one another. This chapter looks at how to use layers to expand your creative possibilities.

120 Layering Images

121 Layers Panel

122 Adding Layers

123 Fill and Adjustment Layers

125 Working with Layers

126 Layer Masks

129 Opacity

130 Saving Layers

Layering Images

Layering is a technique that enables you to add additional elements to an image, and place them on separate layers, so that they can be edited and manipulated independently from other elements in the image. It is like creating an image using transparent sheets of film: each layer is independent of the others but, when they are combined, a composite image is created. This is an extremely versatile technique for working with digital images.

By using layers, several different elements can be combined to create a composite image:

Original image

Final image
With text, gradient and shapes added (four additional layers have been added).

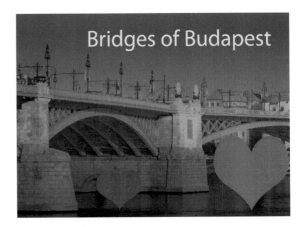

Layers Panel

The use of layers within Elements is done within Expert edit mode and is governed by the Layers panel. When an image is first opened it is shown in the Layers panel as the Background layer. While this remains as the Background layer it cannot be moved above any other layers. However, it can be converted into a normal layer, in which case it operates in the same way as any other layer. To convert a Background layer into a normal one:

1 Click on the **Layers** button on the Taskbar

2 The open image is shown in the Layers panel as the Background

3 Double-click on the layer. Enter a name for it and click on the **OK** button

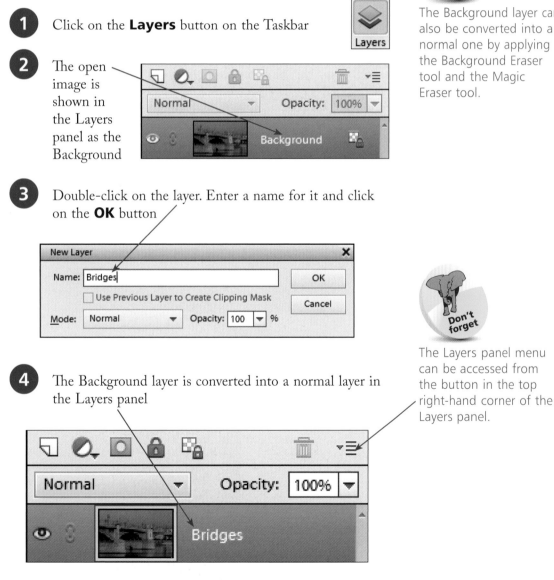

4 The Background layer is converted into a normal layer in the Layers panel

Hot tip

The Background layer can also be converted into a normal one by applying the Background Eraser tool and the Magic Eraser tool.

Don't forget

The Layers panel menu can be accessed from the button in the top right-hand corner of the Layers panel.

Adding Layers

New blank layers can be added whenever you want to include new content within an image. This could be part of another image that has been copied and pasted, a whole new image, text or an object. To add a new layer:

1 Click here on the Layers panel

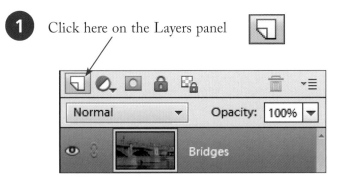

2 Double-click on the layer name and overtype to give the layer a new name

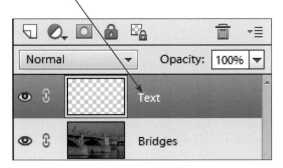

3 With the new layer selected in the Layers panel, add content to the layer. This will be visible over the layer, or layers, below it

Fill and Adjustment Layers

Fill and adjustment layers can be added to images to give an effect behind or above the main subject. To do this:

 Open the Layers panel and select a layer. The fill or adjustment layer will be placed directly above the selected layer

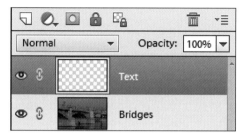

Click here at the bottom of the Layers panel

 Select one of the fill or adjustment options. The fill options are **Solid Color, Gradient** or **Pattern Fill**

Solid Color...
Gradient...
Pattern...

Levels...
Brightness/Contrast...

Hue/Saturation...
Gradient Map...
Photo Filter...

Invert
Threshold...
Posterize...

Beware

For a Fill layer to be visible behind the main image, the image must have a transparent background. To achieve this, select the main subject. Choose **Select > Inverse** from the Menu bar and press the **Delete** key to delete the background. A checkerboard effect should be visible, which denotes that this part of the image is transparent. This only works on layers that have been converted into normal layers, rather than the Background one.

Don't forget

The Adjustments panel is used for Levels, Brightness/Contrast, Hue/Saturation, Gradient Map, Photo Filter, Threshold and Posterize.

123

...cont'd

 4 For a Solid Color, Gradient or Pattern Fill, the required fill is selected from a dialog box and this is added to the selected layer

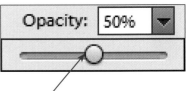

 5 For an adjustment option, settings can be applied within the Adjustments panel

 6 Once fill and adjustment settings have been applied, the effect can be edited by changing the opacity. This is done by dragging this slider

 **7** The opacity level determines how much of the image is visible through the fill or adjustment layer

Working with Layers

Moving layers

The order in which layers are arranged in the Layers panel is known as the stacking order. It is possible to change a layer's position in the stacking order, which affects how it is viewed in the composite image. To do this:

1 Click and drag a layer within the Layers panel to change its stacking order

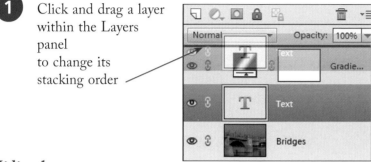

Beware

Layers can be deleted by selecting them and clicking on the Trashcan icon in the Layers panel. However, this also deletes all of the content on that layer.

Hiding layers

Layers can be hidden while you are working on other parts of an image. However, the layer is still part of the composite image – it has not been removed. To hide a layer:

1 Click here so that a line appears through the eye icon. Click again to remove the line and reveal the layer

Locking layers

Layers can be locked, so that they cannot be edited accidentally while you are working on other parts of an image. To do this:

1 Select a layer and click here so that the padlock is activated. The padlock also appears on the layer

Layer Masks

Because layers can be separated within an individual image there is a certain amount of versatility, in terms of how different layers can interact with each other. One of these ways is to create a layer mask. This is a top-level layer, through which an area is removed so that the layer below is revealed. To do this:

 Open an image. It will be displayed as the Background in the Layers panel. Double-click on this to select it

 Give the layer a new name and click on the **OK** button

126

Different types of content can be added as the top layer in an image to be used as a layers mask. Whatever is added has to be converted to a normal layer rather than a background one.

 Click on the **Graphics** button on the Taskbar to access the Graphics panel

Graphics

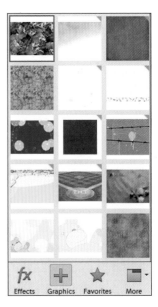

Select a
background
and double-
click on it
to add it to
the current
image.
Initially, this
is added
below the open image. Rename the new layer

 Drag the
added layer
above the
original
image (this
can also
be done by
selecting
an area in
another image, copying it and then pasting it above the
existing image)

Beware

Make sure that all layers
are converted into
normal layers, rather
than background ones.

6 The background image now covers the original one

...cont'd

7 Click here to apply a layer mask to the top layer

8 Select either one of the **Marquee** tools, the **Lasso** tools, or the **Brush** tool from the Toolbox

128

9 Select an area on the top layer and delete it to display the image below it (**Edit > Delete** from the Menu bar)

10 In the Layers panel, the area that has been removed is displayed here

Opacity

The opacity of a layer can be set to determine how much of the layer below is visible through the selected layer. To do this:

1 Select a layer either in the Layers panel or by clicking on the relevant item within an image

2 Click here and drag the slider to achieve the required level of opacity. The greater the amount of opacity, the less transparent the selected layer becomes

3 The opacity setting determines how much of the background, or the layer below, is visible through the selected one and this can be used to create some interesting artistic effects, including a watermark effect if the opacity is applied to a single layer with nothing behind it

Hot tip

The background behind an image, to which opacity has been applied, can be changed within the Preferences section by selecting **Edit > Preferences** from the Menu bar and then selecting **Transparency** and editing the items in the Grid Colors box.

129

Saving Layers

Once an image has been created using two or more layers, there are two ways in which the composite image can be saved: in a proprietary Photoshop format, in which case individual layers are maintained, or in a general file format, where all of the layers will be merged into a single one. The advantage of the former is that individual elements can still be edited within the image, independently of other items. In general, it is good practice to save layered images in both a Photoshop and a non-Photoshop format. To save layered images in a Photoshop format:

Hot tip

Before a layer is saved it is possible to create a composite image consisting of a single layer. To do this, select **Layer > Flatten Image** from the Menu bar. To merge the existing layer and the one below it, select **Layer > Merge Down** from the Menu bar, and to merge all visible content (excluding any layers that have been hidden) select **Layer > Merge Visible**.

1 Select **File > Save As** from the Menu bar

2 Make sure Photoshop (*.PSD, *.PDD) is selected as the format

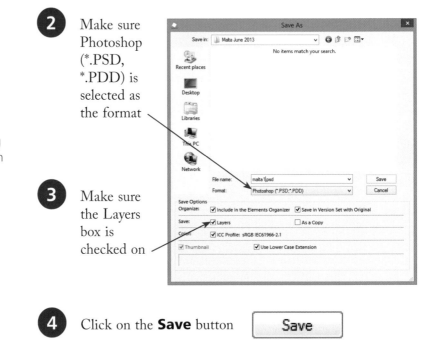

3 Make sure the Layers box is checked on

4 Click on the **Save** button

Beware

Layered images that are saved in the Photoshop PSD/PDD format can increase dramatically in file size, compared with the original image or a layered image that has been flattened.

To save in a non-Photoshop format, select **File > Save As** from the Menu bar. Select the file format from the Format box (such as JPEG or TIFF) and click on the **Save** button. The Layers box will not be available.

8

Text and Drawing Tools

Elements offers a lot more than just the ability to edit digital images. It also has options for adding and formatting text and creating a variety of graphical objects. This chapter looks at how to add text and also includes drawing objects.

132 Adding and Formatting Text

134 Customizing Text

138 Distorting Text

139 Text and Shape Masks

141 Adding Shapes

142 Paint Bucket Tool

143 Gradient Tool

145 Brush and Pencil Tools

146 Impressionist Brush Tool

147 Working with Color

Adding and Formatting Text

Text can be added to images in Elements and this can be used to create a wide range of items, such as cards, brochures and posters. To add text to an image:

Beware

Use the Vertical Type tool sparingly, as this is not a natural way for the eye to read text. Use it with small amounts of text, for effect.

Don't forget

Anti-aliasing is a technique that smooths out the jagged edges that can sometimes appear with text when viewed on a computer monitor. Anti-aliasing is created by adding pixels to the edges of text, so that it blends more smoothly with the background.

1 Select the **Horizontal** or **Vertical Type** tool from the Toolbox

2 Drag on the image with the Type tool to create a text box

3 Make the required formatting selections from the Tool Options panel

Type tools   Font type   Font size

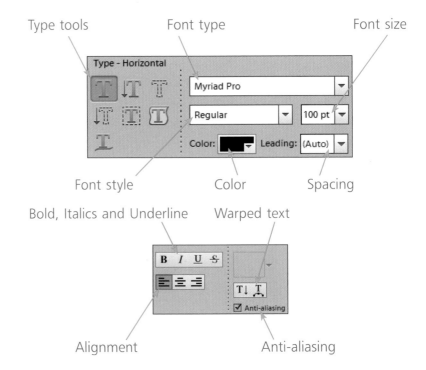

Font style   Color   Spacing

Bold, Italics and Underline   Warped text

Alignment   Anti-aliasing

4 Type the
text onto
the image.
This is
automatically
placed on as
a new layer
at the top of
the stacking
order in the Layers panel

5 To move the
text, select
it with the
Move tool,
click and
drag it to a
new position

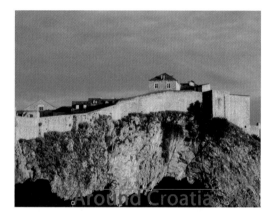

To format text that has already been entered:

1 Select a **Type**
tool and drag it
over a piece of
text to select it

2 Make the
changes in the
Tool Options
panel, as shown in Step 3 on the facing page

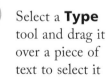

3 Click on the green tick to accept the
text entry

Customizing Text

As well as adding standard text, it is also possible to add text to follow a selection, a shape or a custom path. This can be done within Expert edit and Quick edit modes.

Adding text to a selection
To add text to a selection within an image:

 Click on the **Type** tool and select the **Text on Selection** tool option

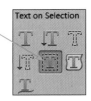

 Drag over an area of an image to make a selection

Don't forget

In Expert edit mode, select the Move tool and click and drag the text to move it and also the selection area.

 Click on the green tick to accept the selection

4 Click anywhere on the selection and add text. By default, this will be displayed along the outside of the selection

 Format the text in the same way as with standard text

Adding text to a shape

To add text to a shape within an image:

1 Click on the **Type** tool and select the **Text on Shape** tool option

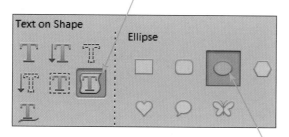

2 Click here in the Tool Options panel to select a shape

3 Drag over an area of an image to create a shape

Hot tip

Once customized text has been added and accepted it can still be edited in the same way as standard text, by using the Horizontal Type Tool and selecting the customized text.

4 Click anywhere on the shape and add text. Click on the green tick as in Step 3 on the previous page

5 Format the text in the same way as with standard text

...cont'd

Adding text to a custom path

Text can also be added to a custom path that you draw on an image. To do this:

 Open the image onto which you want to create text on a custom path

The Modify button is used to edit an existing text path, see next page.

 Click on the **Type** tool and select the **Text on Custom Path** tool option. Make sure the **Draw** button is also selected

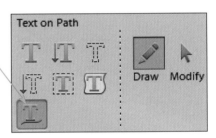

Draw a custom path on the image

4 Click on the green tick to accept the text path

5 Click anywhere on the custom path and add text

6 Format the text in the same way as with standard text

Myriad Pro		▼	Color:	▼
Regular	▼	48 pt	▼	

7 Click on the **Modify** tool in the Tool Options panel. This activates the markers along the custom path

8 Drag the markers to move the position of the custom path

Beware

If there is too much text on a custom path it can become jumbled, particularly if you adjust the markers on the path.

9 The custom path can be used to position text in a variety of ways around objects or people

Distorting Text

In addition to producing standard text, it is also possible to create some dramatic effects by distorting text. To do this:

It is possible to select the distort options once a text tool has been selected but before the text is added.

1 Enter plain text and select it by dragging a **Type** tool over it

2 Click the **Create Warped Text** button on the Tool Options panel

3 Click here and select one of the options in the Warp Text dialog box. Click on the **OK** button

Warp Text	✕
Style: None ▼	OK
	Cancel
None	
Bend: ⌒ Arc %	
⌓ Arc Lower	
⌒ Arc Upper	
Horizont ⌒ Arch %	
⊖ Bulge	
Vertical ⌓ Shell Lower %	
⌒ Shell Upper	

4 The selected effect is applied to the text

Use text distortion sparingly, as it can become annoying if it is overdone.

Text and Shape Masks

Text Masks can be used to reveal an area of an image showing through the text. This can be used to produce eye-catching headings and slogans. To do this:

1 Select the **Horizontal** or **Vertical Type Mask** tool from the Toolbox

2 Click on an image, then enter and format text as you would for normal text. A red mask is applied to the image when the mask text is entered

Text Mask effects work best if the text used is fairly large in size. In some cases it is a good idea to use bold text, as this is wider than standard text.

3 Press **Enter** or click the **Move** tool to border the mask text with dots

...cont'd

 Select **Edit > Copy** from the Menu bar

 Select **File > New** from the Menu bar and create a new file

 Select **Edit > Paste** from the Menu bar to paste the text mask into the new file

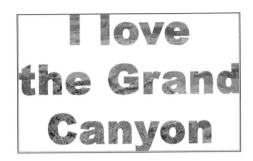

140

Cookie Cutter masks

A similar effect can be created with shape masks by using the Cookie Cutter tool (grouped with the Crop tool):

 Select the **Cookie Cutter** tool in the Toolbox and click here to select a particular style in the Tool Options panel

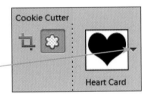

Drag on an image to create a cut-out effect

Adding Shapes

Another way to add extra style to your images is through the use of shapes. There are several types of symmetrical shapes that can be added to images, and also a range of custom ones. To add shapes to an image:

1 Click on the **Custom Shape** tool and select the type of shape you want to create

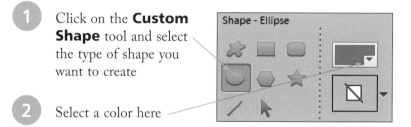

2 Select a color here

3 Click and drag on the image to create the selected shape

4 If you want to change the color of a shape, click here in the Tool Options panel and select a new color. This can either be done before the shape is created or it can be used to edit the color of an existing shape, when selected with the **Move** tool

Paint Bucket Tool

The Paint Bucket tool can be used to add a solid color to a selection or an area in an image. To do this:

For more information on working with color, see pages 147-148.

The higher the tolerance, the greater the area to which the color is applied with the Paint Bucket tool.

1 Open the image to which you want to apply the Paint Bucket

2 Select the **Paint Bucket** tool from the Toolbox

3 Select the **Opacity** and **Tolerance** in the Tool Options panel. The Tolerance determines how much of an image is affected by the Paint Bucket

4 Click once on an area of solid color with the Paint Bucket tool. The color in Step 2 will be applied

Gradient Tool

The Gradient tool can be used to add a gradient fill to a selection or an entire image. To do this:

1 Select an area in an image or select an object

Beware

If no selection is made for a gradient fill, the effect will be applied to the entire selected layer.

2 Select the **Gradient** tool from the Toolbox

Gradient

Edit...

3 Click here in the Tool Options panel to select pre-set gradient fills

4 Click on a gradient style to apply it as the default

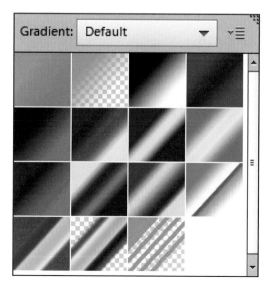

Gradient: Default

Hot tip

The default gradient effect in the Tool Options panel is created with the currently-selected foreground and background colors within the Toolbox.

...cont'd

5 Click here in the Tool Options panel to access the **Gradient Editor** dialog box

To create a new pre-set gradient, create it in the Gradient Editor dialog box and click on the **Add to Preset** button to add it to the list of pre-set gradients. Click on the gradient's icon to give it a unique name in the **Name** box.

6 Click and drag the sliders to change the amount of a particular color in the gradient

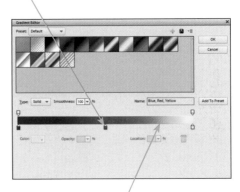

7 Click along here to add a new color marker. Click on the **OK** button

8 Click an icon in the Tool Options bar to select a gradient style

The amount that the cursor is dragged, when adding a gradient, determines where the centerpoint of the gradient is located and also the size of each segment of the gradient.

9 Click and drag within the original selection to specify the start and end points of the gradient effect

Brush and Pencil Tools

The Brush and Pencil tools work in a similar way and can be used to create lines of varying thickness and style. To do this:

1 Select the **Brush** tool or the **Pencil** tool from the Toolbox

2 Select the required options from the Tool Options panel

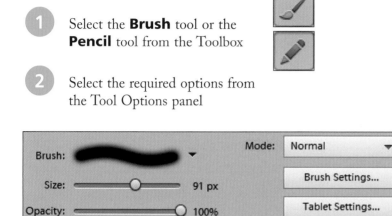

3 Click and drag to create lines on an image. (The lines are placed directly on the image. To add lines without altering the background image, add a new layer above the background and add the lines on this layer. They will then be visible over the background.)

The Mode options for the Brush and Pencil tools are similar to those for blending layers together. They include options such as Darken, Lighten, Soft Light and Difference. Each of these enables the line to blend with the image below it.

The Brush and Pencil tools are very similar in the way they function, except that the Brush tool has more options and can create more subtle effects.

Impressionist Brush Tool

The Impressionist Brush tool can be used to create a dappled effect over an image, similar to that of an impressionist painting. To do this:

 Select the **Impressionist Brush** tool from the Toolbox

 Select the required options from the Tool Options panel

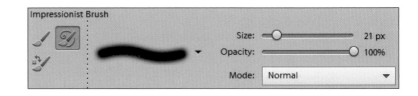

3 Click and drag over an image to create an impressionist effect

If the brush size is too large for the Impressionist Brush tool, it can result in the effect being too extreme and a lot of definition being lost in an image.

Working with Color

All of the text and drawing tools make extensive use of color. Elements provides a number of methods for selecting colors, and also for working with them.

Foreground and background colors

At the bottom of the Toolbox there are two colored squares. These represent the currently-selected foreground and background colors. The foreground color, which is the most frequently used, is the one that is applied to drawing objects, such as fills and lines, and also text. The background color is used for items, such as gradient fills, and for areas that have been removed with the Eraser tool.

Foreground color   Swap foreground and background colors

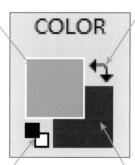

Set foreground to black and background to white   Background color

Hot tip

Whenever the foreground or background color squares are clicked on, the Eyedropper tool is automatically activated. This can be used to select a color from anywhere on your screen, instead of using the Color Picker.

147

Color Picker

The Color Picker can be used to select a new color for the foreground or background color. To do this:

1   Click once on the foreground or the background color square, as required

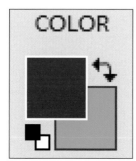

...cont'd

If you are going to be using images on the Web, check on the **Only Web Colors** box. This will display a different range of colors, which are known as web-safe colors. This means that they will appear the same on any type of web browser.

② In the Color Picker, click to select a color

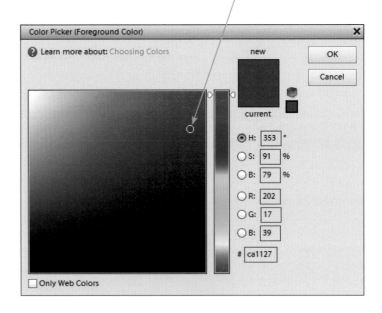

③ Click on the **OK** button

When the cursor is moved over a color in the Color Swatches panel, the tooltip displays a description of the color, e.g. RGB Green, or Pastel Red.

Color Swatches panel

The Color Swatches panel can be used to access different color panels that can then be used to select the foreground and background colors. To do this:

① Select **Window > Color Swatches** from the Menu bar

② Click here to access the available panels

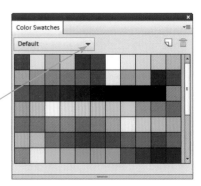

9 Artistic Effects

Adding special effects is one of the fun and creative things you can do with digital images. This chapter shows how to create stunning effects, to give your photos the "wow" factor.

150 About Graphics and Effects

152 Adding Filters

154 Zoom Burst

156 Depth of Field

158 Photo Puzzles

160 Out of Bounds

163 Black and White Selection

164 Reflections

About Graphics and Effects

Applying artistic effects can be one of the most satisfying parts of digital image editing: it is quick and the results can be dramatic. Elements has a range of Graphics and Effects that can be applied to images. To use these:

 In Expert edit mode, click on the **Graphics** button

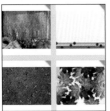

 Within the Graphics panel click here to select a category for a particular topic

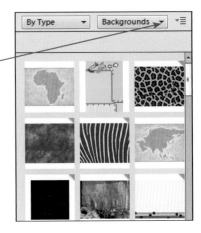

Click here to see all of the options for a particular category. Double-click on an item in the Graphics panel to add it to the currently-active image

Accessing Effects

To apply special effects to an open image in the Editor:

 In Expert edit mode, click on the **Effects** button

 Select the required effect in the Effects panel. Double-click to apply it to the currently-active image

Some effects, such as Filters, have additional dialog boxes (see page 152) in which a variety of settings can be specified in relation to how the effect operates and appears. For others, the effect is applied immediately

The range of effects have been updated in Elements 13.

In Quick and Guided edit modes, the filters can be accessed from the **Filter** menu on the Menu bar.

Many of the items in the Effects panel can be applied by double-clicking on them, or dragging them onto the image.

Adding Filters

As shown on the previous page, filters can be accessed from the Effects panel in Expert edit mode. They can also be accessed and applied from the Menu bar in any of the Editor modes. To add and modify filters:

 In any of the Editor modes, open the photo to which you want to apply a filter effect

 Select **Filter** from the Menu bar and select one of the filter categories and sub-categories

 Some filter effects have a dialog box where additional settings can be applied

4 Click on one of the Presets options to apply this automatically to the photo

 5 Drag these sliders to increase or decrease the amount of color for the selected filter effect

 6 Drag this slider to increase or decrease the size of lines for the selected filter effect

7 Click on the **OK** button

8 The filter effect is applied to the photo

Don't forget

The Comic and Graphic Novel filters are the ones that have the outline thickness option shown in Step 6. These are both found under the **Filters > Sketch** category.

153

Zoom Burst

The Zoom Burst effect is a very dramatic one that can create a sense of motion and vibrancy in a photo.

 1 Open the image to which you want to add the zoom burst effect. It is most effective to use one that has a sense of drama or motion

Hot tip

In the Photo Effects section there are options for changing parts of a photo to black and white, create a line drawing effect and create an old fashioned photo effect.

 2 Access Guided edit mode. In the **Camera Effects** section, click on the **Zoom Burst Effect** button

 3 Click on the **Crop** button to crop the image so that the main subject is in the center, if required

1. Use the Crop Tool to crop your image so that the primary subject is in the center.

Crop Tool

4 Click on the **Add Zoom Burst** button to apply the zoom burst effect to the photo

2. Click the Add Zoom Burst button to apply the effect to your image. Press multiple times to increase the effect.

Add Zoom Burst

5 Click on the **Add Focus Area** button and drag on the area of the image that you want to remain in focus. The rest of the image will retain the zoom burst effect

3. Click the Add Focus Area button and then click and drag on your image to specify the area of focus. Repeat as needed to increase the area of focus.

Add Focus Area

Don't forget

Apply the Add Zoom Burst option more than once to make the effect more dramatic, but be careful not to overdo it.

6 Click on the **Apply Vignette** button and apply a vignette effect which creates a dark, shadow border around the image

4. [Optional] Add Vignette to your image. Click the button again to intensify the effect.

Apply Vignette

7 Click on the **Done** button to complete the zoom burst effect

Done

Depth of Field

Depth of field is a photographic technique where part of a photo is deliberately blurred, for artistic effect. Traditionally, this has been done through camera settings, but in Elements the same effect can be created within the Guided edit mode. To do this:

Hot tip

A similar effect to depth of field can be achieved with the Tilt-Shift Guided edit option.

156

 Open the image to which you want to add the depth of field effect

 Access Guided edit mode. In the **Camera Effects** section, click on the **Depth of Field** button

 Click on the **Simple** button

 Click on the **Add Blur** button to add a blurred effect to the whole image

5 Click on the
Add Focus Area button

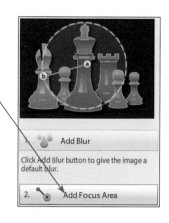

 6 Drag on the image, covering the
area that you want to appear in focus

Hot tip

The most realistic depth of field effect is done by dragging the **Add Focus Area** tool from front to back, in a straight line. It can also be done diagonally, but this is not something that could easily be achieved with a camera.

157

7 Drag this slider to increase the amount of blur of the area that is not in focus

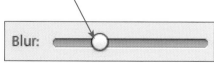

8 Click on the **Done** button

Photo Puzzles

The Photo Play effects are very creative and the Puzzle Effect lets you create jigsaw effects out of your photos:

 Open the image to which you want to add the jigsaw effect

Two types of photographic effects can be added to photos under Photo Effects in Guided edit mode. These are the Lomo Camera Effect which puts a vignette around an image and creates a more vibrantly colored image. The Orton Effect gives a soft-focus appearance to a photo.

 Access Guided edit mode. In the **Photo Play** section, click on the **Puzzle Effect** button

Photo Play

- Out Of Bounds
- Picture Stack
- Pop Art
- Puzzle Effect

 Select a size for the pieces of the jigsaw

Puzzle Effect

After (Roll over to see Before)

1. Click on one of the buttons below to give your image a Puzzle Effect.

Small   Medium   Large

4 Click on the **Select Puzzle Piece** button and click on a piece of the jigsaw to select it

2. Enhance the effect by extracting a puzzle piece.

2a. Click the Select Puzzle Piece button, and then click on the center of any puzzle piece.

Select Puzzle Piece

5 Click on the **Extract Piece** button to remove the piece from the jigsaw

Select Puzzle Piece

2b. Click on the Extract Piece button to extract your selected puzzle piece.

Extract Piece

Don't forget

Photo Puzzles are still just photos: the effect does not create an actual jigsaw.

6 Click on the **Move Tool** button and select a piece to move and rotate it

3. Use the Move tool to arrange the extracted piece.

Move Tool

7 Repeat Steps 4, 5 and 6 until you have the appearance of a jigsaw being completed

Out of Bounds

Another effective special effect in Elements is called Out of Bounds. This can be used to display a section of an image without the rest of the original photo. This works best when there is one part of the image that obviously sticks out from the rest, such as part of a building, or someone's arm or leg. To do this:

Don't forget

As long as it is a defined area, anything can be used to appear without the rest of the image.

 Open an image that has an element that will naturally stick out from the rest

 Access Guided edit mode. In the **Photo Play** section, click on the **Out Of Bounds** button

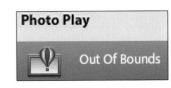

 Click on the **Add Frame** button

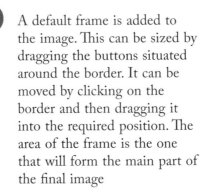

A default frame is added to the image. This can be sized by dragging the buttons situated around the border. It can be moved by clicking on the border and then dragging it into the required position. The area of the frame is the one that will form the main part of the final image

5 Hold down
Shift + Ctrl + Alt
to add perspective to the
frame. This can be done
by dragging the corner
buttons and also those in
the middle of each side

6 Click on the green arrow to apply the
changes to the frame

7 The frame is displayed,
with the rest of
the image grayed-out

8 Click on the **Selection
Tool** button

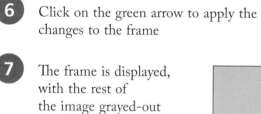

The frame contains the
area that will be the
main part of the image,
not the Out of Bounds
selection.

9 Drag over the area that will appear
outside the main image

...cont'd

 Click on the **Out of Bounds Effect** button

 The area selected in Step 9 now appears on its own, outside the area created by the frame

Hot tip

Zoom in on the area to be selected so that you can do this with greater precision and accuracy.

 Click on the **Add Background Gradient** button to add a background gradient to the final image

 Click on one of the **Add Shadow** buttons to add a drop shadow to the image

Click on the **Done** button to complete the process and display the Out of Bounds image

Black and White Selection

A popular photo effect is to make part of an image black and white and leave one element in color. To do this:

1 Open an image to which you want to apply the black and white effect

2 Access Guided edit mode. In the **Photo Effects** section, click on the **B&W Selection** button

3 Click on the **B&W Selection Brush** button and drag it over the area you want to select

The selection brush in Step 3 is the quick selection brush, which selects areas of similar color as you drag it over the image.

4 Click on the **Add** or **Subtract** buttons to add or remove areas of the selection

5 The area selected will be in black and white. To leave it in color and make the rest of the image black and white, check **On** the **Invert Effect** button. Click on the **Done** button to complete the black and white process

Reflections

Reflections of an image can be one of the most satisfying photographic effects. Images reflected in water, or on a clear surface, can create a very artistic and calming effect. However, it can be difficult to get the perfect reflection when taking an original photo. To help overcome this Elements has a Guided edit that can create the effect for you. To do this:

Beware

If you select an image that does not have enough detail in the foreground, the join with the reflected image may appear too severe and slightly unnatural.

1 Open the image you want to use for the reflection. If possible, use one with some objects in the foreground

2 Access Guided edit mode. In the **Photo Play** section, click on the **Reflection** button

3 Click on the **Add Reflection** button

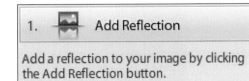

4 The reflection effect is applied to the image

 5 Depending on the type of reflection you are creating you can add a background color by selecting the **Eyedropper Tool** button and clicking on the **Fill Background** button

If a background color is used, this will be applied to the reflected image. However, this step does not have to be used.

6 Select the type of reflection effect you want to create

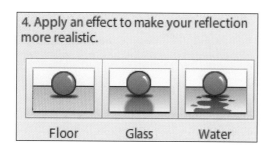

...cont'd

When an effect is
applied, it looks more
defined the more that
you zoom in on an
image. To see it in its
normal state it is best to
view the image at 1:1,
i.e. 100%.

 Each option has
different dialog boxes
which can be used to
set the amount. Click
on the **OK** button to
apply the selected effect

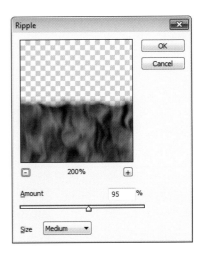

 The effect is applied to
the reflected half of the
image

 Additional options can be
applied to fine-tune the selected
effect further

 Click on the **Done** button to
complete the process

Done

10 Sharing and Creating

This chapter shows how you can share images creatively and also use and edit them in artistic projects.

168   About Share Mode

170   Mobile Sharing

172   Sharing with Adobe Revel

173   About Create Mode

177   Facebook Covers

About Share Mode

Share mode enables you to output your images in a variety of ways, and also send them to friends and family in different formats. Some of these involve third-party services and these will vary depending on your own location. Also, some of the options offered through the Share mode require the video-editing program, Elements Premiere. The standard options within Share mode are:

- **Private Web Album.** This is an app that can be used to share your photos. Elements can share photos directly with Adobe Revel, see pages 170-172.

- **Share to Flickr, Twitter and Facebook.** This can be used to share images to these popular social media sites.

- **Email.** This can be used to attach photos to emails via your email program.

- **Vimeo.** This is an online video-sharing service, where your Elements videos can be shared and viewed.

- **YouTube.** This can be used to upload videos to YouTube.

- **Burn Video DVD/ BluRay.** This requires Elements Premiere.

- **PDF Slideshow.** This creates a slide show in PDF format which means that it should be possible to open it on most computers.

To use Share mode

1 In either the Editor or the Organizer, click on the **Share** tab and select an option

2 Add content to be shared (either by selecting it initially or by dragging it into the content panel)

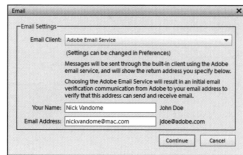

3 Some of the Share options require a form of registration for the selected option

4 Format the content using the wizards and templates within the Share section. Click on the **Next** button to move through the wizards and templates. Click on the **Done** button to complete the process and share your photos with the selected Share option

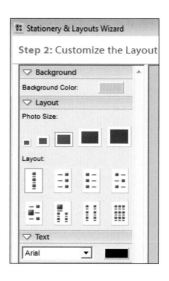

Each Share option has a slightly different wizard, but the basic process is the same for each one.

Mobile Sharing

With the proliferation of mobile devices (such as smartphones and tablets) now in widespread use, people want their favorite items to be available on all of their devices, whenever they want. Elements 13 fulfils this need through the use of mobile albums that can be viewed with the online Adobe Revel service. This can be used with an Adobe ID (which is free to create) and once you have done this you can upload your photos from within Elements 13 and then use Adobe Revel to view them and, if desired, add to them on the move. To do this:

1 Open the **Organizer**

2 In the folders and albums panel, click on the **Mobile Albums** button

▶ Mobile Albums   ⓘ

3 You will be prompted to log in with your Adobe ID, or create a new one if you do not have one. Follow the wizard to log in and set up access to Adobe Revel

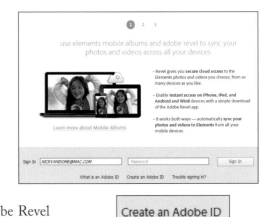

Create an Adobe ID

4 In the folders and albums panel, click on this button next to Mobile Albums and click on **Create New Album**

5   Give the album a name

New Album

Album Name:
Malta
Library:
Nick's Library ▼

6   Click on the **OK** button   OK

7   In the Organizer **Media** window, select the photos that you want to upload to your mobile album

8   Drag the photos into the mobile album that was created in Steps 4, 5 and 6

9   Move the cursor over the album name and click on the **Share** button

10   Click on the **Start Sharing** button

Album Web Share
Web Link:
http://adoberevel.com/shares/7040e22024b54b969eba8d699ee3eb23
☐ Allow Downloads
Copy this Link   Stop Sharing

11   The photos will be visible in your Adobe Revel album (see next page)

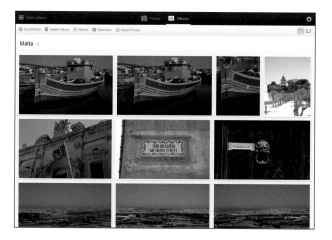

Don't forget

When a new album is created it appears under the Mobile Albums section in the left-hand panel. This is where photos can be placed for sharing online.

▼ Mobile Albums   ➕▾
  ▼ Nick's Library
    🖼 Malta
    🖼 Paris

Hot tip

The link in Step 10 can be copied and sent to other people so that they can use it to access the mobile album.

Sharing with Adobe Revel

Once you have shared photos with a mobile album you can then view them online at the Adobe Revel website. This can be done in a number of ways:

Don't forget

Adobe Revel apps on iPad/iPhone or Windows 8.1 devices can have albums and photos added to them and these will appear on all of your devices with Adobe Revel and also in your Mobile Albums in the Organizer in Elements 13.

Hot tip

In addition to sharing albums from Elements 13 when they are uploaded to Adobe Revel, they can also be shared from within Adobe Revel, by clicking on this icon within an album and selecting an option for sharing.

1. From your computer, access the website at **www. adoberevel.com** and click on the **Sign In** button or the **Sign Up** button

2. On an iPad or iPhone, download the Adobe Revel app from the App Store and log in using your Adobe ID

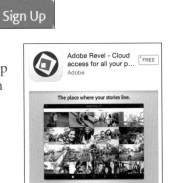

3. On a Windows 8.1 tablet or smartphone, download the Adobe Revel app from the Windows Store and log in using your Adobe ID

4. On an Android tablet or smartphone, access the Adobe Revel website through a browser and log in using your Adobe ID

5. Whichever way you access Adobe Revel, you will be able to view your photos and albums that have been uploaded

About Create Mode

Image-editing programs have now evolved to a point where there is almost as much emphasis on using images creatively as there is on editing them. Elements has an excellent range of options for displaying your images in some stunningly creative ways, called, appropriately enough, Create mode. These can be saved in the Organizer for viewing or sharing. The standard options within Create mode are:

- **Photo Prints.** This can be used to print photos locally on your own printer, or using an online service.

- **Photo Book.** This creates a selection of formatted images that can be printed in a presentational book.

- **Greeting Card.** This creates your own personalized cards.

- **Photo Calendar.** This creates your own personalized calendars.

- **Photo Collage.** This can be used to assemble several images.

- **Facebook Cover.** This creates a photo montage that can be used with a Facebook account. See pages 177-178.

- **Instant Movie.** This requires Elements Premiere.

- **DVD with Menu.** This requires Elements Premiere and can be used to create a DVD of your photos and videos.

- **CD and DVD Jacket.** This can be used to create customized CD and DVD covers.

- **CD and DVD Label.** This can be used to create customized CD and DVD labels.

- **Slideshow.** This creates a slide show of selected images.

To use Create mode:

 In either the Editor or the Organizer, click on the **Create** button

 Select one of the Create options

To only view Create projects in the Organizer, select **Find > By Media Type > Projects** from the Organizer Menu bar.

The Instant Movie and DVD with Menu options are only available from within the Organizer.

In Create mode, Pages, Layouts and Graphics buttons are added to the standard Taskbar.

...cont'd

 In the dialog window for the Create option select a size at which the creation will be printed

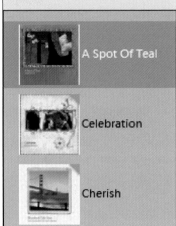

 Select a theme for the creation (this will be applied across the whole creation, even if it has multiple pages). If there is a blue arrow in the top right-hand corner this indicates that this is an online resource which will be downloaded before use

Don't forget

The online themes in Step 4 are downloaded in the same way as the online resources for the backgrounds in the Backgrounds panel, i.e. when they are selected for use they are downloaded to your computer.

 A preview of the layout for the creation is shown in the right-hand panel

 Click on the **OK** button   OK

7 If the theme is an online resource (see Step 4) this will be downloaded to Elements

8 The creation project document is created

9 Click on these arrows to move between the pages of the creation

10 Drag this slider to increase and decrease the viewing size of the creation

11 Click on a text block and overtype to create your own text

12 Click on the **Pages** button on the Taskbar and click here to add new pages to the creation

Text blocks can be used to add your own messages to your photos within creations.

175

...cont'd

 13 Click on the **Layouts** button on the Taskbar and select a layout for the way the photos in the creation will appear

 14 Add more photos to the layout by dragging them onto the one of the image placeholders or by clicking on it and selecting a photo

Beware

Because of the amount of content in them, and the format in which they are saved, Creations can have very large file sizes.

15 Click on the **Graphics** button and double-click on a background to add it to the current creation

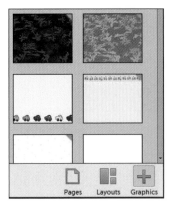

16 Click on the **Save** button to complete the creation. It will then still need to be saved within Elements

Save

 17 Once a project has been saved it is displayed in the Organizer. This means that it can then be opened again and edited if required

| File name: | vacation_holiday_book1|pse | | Save |
| Format: | Photo Project Format (*.PSE) | | Cancel |

Facebook Covers

Facebook is now an established option for many people's day-to-day communications. One item that is used with a Facebook account is a cover photo, which consists of a main timeline photo and a smaller profile picture. These can be created in Facebook itself but Elements also has an option for creating a Facebook Cover, which provides considerable creative options. To do this:

1 Open the photos that you want to use, in the Editor, or select them in the Organizer. Click on the **Create** button and click on the **Facebook Cover** button

2 The options can be selected in the Facebook Cover window. Select a Theme here

Hot tip

When a Facebook Cover is created, it is treated as a Project by Elements.

3 Under the Theme Category, select whether to use a theme with multiple photos or a single one

...cont'd

4 Check **On** the **Autofill with Selected Photos** button to use the photos you have already opened or selected

☑ Autofill with Selected Photos

5 Click on the **OK** button

OK

6 The cover photo is created as a new, composite, image

Hot tip

When a new project has been started using the Create options, click on the **Advanced Mode** button in the top left-hand corner of the window to access the full toolbox and also the Layers panel to view and edit all of the individual elements of the project.

Advanced Mode

7 Use these button to, from left to right: upload the cover image to your Facebook account; save it and continue working on it; or close it

Upload   Save   Close

8 Use these button to, from top to bottom: zoom in on the cover image; move around it; select items within it; and add text to it

Hot tip

Use the Text tool to customize your cover photo and make it even more individual.

11 Printing Images

This chapter shows how to size images for printing, and how to print them in a variety of formats.

180 Print Size

181 Print Functions

183 Print Layouts

185 Online Prints

186 Creating PDF Files

The higher the resolution in the Document Size section of the dialog, the greater the quality, but the smaller the size of the printed image.

180

The output size for a printed image can be worked out by dividing the pixel dimensions (the width and height) by the resolution. So if the width is 2560, the height 1920 and the resolution 300 PPI, the printed image will be approximately 8 inches by 6 inches.

As long as the Resample box is unchecked, changing the output resolution has no effect on the actual number of pixels in an image.

Print Size

Before you start printing images in Elements, it is important to ensure that they are going to be produced at the required size. Since the pixels within an image are not a set size, the printed dimensions of an image can be altered according to your needs. This is done by specifying how many pixels are used within each inch of the image. The more pixels per inch (PPI) then the higher the quality of the printed image, but the smaller in size it will be.

To set the print size of an image (in any of the Editor modes):

1 Open an image and select **Image > Resize> Image Size** from the Menu bar

2 Uncheck the **Resample Image** box. This will ensure that the physical image size, i.e. the number of pixels in the image, remains unchanged when the resolution is changed

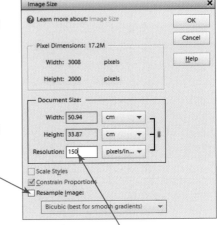

3 The current resolution and document size (print size) are displayed here

4 Enter a new figure in the Resolution box (here, the resolution has been increased from 150 to 300). This affects the Document size, i.e. the size at which the image prints

Document Size:		
Width:	25.47	cm
Height:	16.93	cm
Resolution:	300	pixels/in...

Print Functions

The Print functions in Elements can be accessed from the Menu bar in either the Editor or the Organizer, by selecting **File > Print**. Also, all of the print functions can be selected from Create mode. To print to your local printer using this method:

 Select an image in either the Editor or the Organizer, click on the **Create** button and click on the **Photo Prints** button

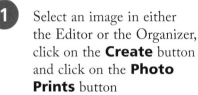

 Click on the **Local Printer** button

Photo Prints

Local Printer

3 The main print window displays the default option for how the printed image will appear and also options for changing the properties of the print

The currently-active images are shown in the left-hand panel of the Print window.

Don't forget

181

4 Click the **Add** button to include more images in the current print job, or select an image and click on the **Remove** button to exclude it

...cont'd

Hot tip

Check on the **Center Image** box in Step 5 to have the image printed in the center of the page.

 Use these options to rotate an image for printing, change its size, or position

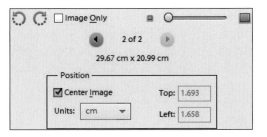

 Click here to select a destination printer to which you want to send your print

Select Printer:

Dell Laser Printer 1720dn (C... ▼

 Click on the **Change Settings** button to change the properties for your own local printer

Printer Settings:

Paper Type: Printer Setting
Print Quality: 600 DPI
Tray: Automatically Select

Change Settings...

8 Click here to select the paper size for printing

Select Paper Size:

A4 ▼

Orientation:

9 Click here to select the print type, i.e. the layout of the image you are printing

Select Type of Print:

Individual Prints ▼

10 Click here to select the size at which you want your image to be printed

Select Print Size:

Actual Size (25.47cm x 16.9... ▼

☐ Crop to Fit

11 Click on the **Print** button to print your image with the settings selected above

 Print...

Print Layouts

Rather than just offering the sole function of printing a single image on a sheet of paper, Elements has two options that can be used when printing images, which can help reduce the number of sheets of paper used.

Picture Package

This can be used to print out copies of different images on a single piece of paper. To do this:

1 Select an image in either the Editor or the Organizer, click on the Create button and click on the **Picture Package** button

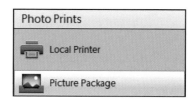

2 The layout for the Picture Package is displayed in the main print window

3 Under **Select a Layout**, select how many images you want on a page and, if required, select a type of frame for the printed images

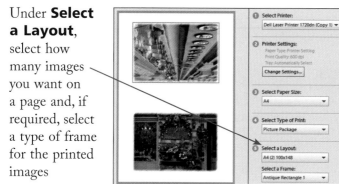

Hot tip

When buying a printer, choose one that has borderless printing. This means that it can print to the very edge of the page. This is particularly useful for items, such as files, produced as a Picture Package.

Don't forget

The Picture Package function is useful for printing images in a combination of sizes, such as for family portraits.

...cont'd

Contact Sheets

This can be used to create and print thumbnail versions of a large number of images. To do this:

 Select an image in either the Editor or the Organizer, click on the Create button and click on the **Contact Sheet** button

 The layout for the Contact Sheet is displayed in the main Print window

Don't forget

When a contact sheet is created, new thumbnail images are generated. The original images are unaffected.

 Click under **Select Type of Print** and select the number of columns to be displayed on the contact sheet

Online Prints

Printing digital images online is now firmly established and is an excellent way of getting high quality, economical prints without leaving the comfort of your own home:

1 Open an image, or images, in either the Editor, or select them in the Organizer. Click on the **Create** button and select Photo Prints. There

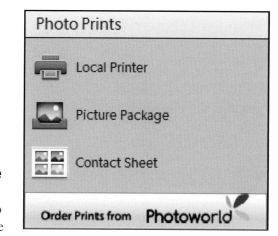

are options for printing images on your own printer, and also services for online prints. These will be specific to your own location

2 When you click on one of the services you will be taken to its website, from where you will be able to order your online prints. You will have to register for the site initially, which will be free. Most services will also have an option for uploading your photos, so that they can also be viewed and shared online

Hot tip

When printing images, either online or on your own printer, make sure that they have been captured at the highest resolution setting on your camera, to ensure the best printed quality.

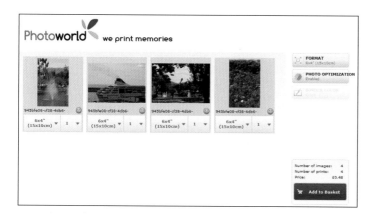

Creating PDF Files

PDF (Portable Document Format) is a file format that is used to maintain the original formatting and style of a document, so that it can be viewed on a variety of different devices and types of computers. In general, it is usually used for documents that contain text and images, such as information pamphlets, magazine features and chapters from books. However, image files, such as JPEGs, can also be converted into PDF and this can be done within Elements without the need for any other special software. To do this:

Don't forget

PDF files are an excellent way to share files so that other people can print them. All that is required is a copy of Adobe Acrobat Reader, which is bundled with most software packages on computers, or can be downloaded from the Adobe website at: www.adobe.com

 Open an image and select **File > Save As** from the Menu bar

 Select a destination folder and make sure the format is set to Photoshop PDF. Then click **Save**

File name:	malta2.pdf	Save
Format:	Photoshop PDF (*.PDF;*.PDP)	Cancel

 The PDF file is created and can be opened in Adobe Acrobat or Elements

Index

A

Abstract colors
    Creating   94
Acrobat Reader   186
Adjustment layers.   See Layers: Adjustment layers
Adjustments panel.   See Panels: Adjustments
Adobe   8, 186
Adobe Revel   170, 172
Albums   48
Artistic effects/techniques   146
Auto Color Correction.
    See Color enhancements: Auto Color Correction
Auto Contrast.   See Color enhancements: Auto Contrast
Auto Levels.   See Color enhancements: Auto Levels
Auto Smart Fix   54

B

Background
    Removing   68
Black and white images
    Converting to   76-77
Black and White Selection   163
Blemishes
    Removing large   62
    Removing small   63
Brightness/Contrast.
    See Color enhancements: Brightness/Contrast
Brush tool   145

C

Camera Effects
    Depth of Field   156-157
    Lomo Camera Effect   158
    Orton Effect   158
    Zoom Burst   154-155
Camera RAW dialog box   100
Cloning   60
CMYK color model
    Not supported   18

Color
    Removing   77
    Web-safe colors   148
    Working with   147-148
Color channels   96
Color enhancements   54, 54-55
    Auto Color Correction   55
    Auto Contrast   54
    Auto Levels   54
    Brightness/Contrast   55
    Shadows/Highlights   56
Color Swatches.   See Panels: Color Swatches
Comic filter   153
Composite images   120
Content-Aware editing   74-75
    Extending   75
Contiguous   68
Covering imperfections   60
Create mode   22
    About   173-174
    CD/DVD Jacket   173
    CD/DVD Label   173
    DVD with Menu   173
    Facebook Cover   173
    Greeting Cards   173
    Instant Movie   173
    Photo Book   173
    Photo Calendar   173
    Photo Collage   173
    Photo Prints   173
    Slideshow   173
Creating effects with text   139
Creations
    Creating   173-176
Cropping   57-59
    Auto Crop   59
    Overlay options   58
    Preset sizes   57
    Rule of Thirds   58

D

Depth of Field.   See Camera Effects: Depth of Field
Digital camera   50
Digital images
    Creating copies for editing purposes   76
    Improving color   54

Increasing and decreasing size   104
Physical size   102
Removing large objects   60
Removing unwanted areas   57
Document size   103
Dodge tool   54
Downloading images   28-29

E

Edges
    Refining   117
Editing areas within an image   106
Edit menu.   See Menu bar: Edit
Editor modes   10
Effects
    Accessing   151
    Adding
        About   150-151
Effects panel.   See Panels: Effects
Elements
    About   8-9
    For the Mac   8
Elements Premiere   51, 168
eLive   10, 24-25
    Inspire   24
    Learn   25
    News   25
Enhance menu.   See Menu bar: Enhance
Eraser tool   68
Erasing a background   68
Events View   21, 40-41
Expert edit mode   10, 14-17

F

Facebook Covers   177-178
Face recognition.   See People View
Face tagging.   See People View
Feathering   115
File formats.   See Image file formats
File menu.   See Menu bar: File
Fill layers.   See Layers: Fill layers
Filters
    Adding   152-153
Finding images   20, 44-47
Folders   49

G

GIF   50
Gradients
    Adding   143-144
Graphic Novel filter   153
Graphics
    Adding   150
Graphics panel.   See Panels: Graphics
Grid   66
Guided edit mode   10, 13, 84-85
    Photo Effects   85
    Photo Play   85
    Touchups   84
    Working with   84

H

Help   26
Help menu.   See Menu bar: Help
Histogram   96-97.   See also Panels: Histogram
History panel.   See Panels: History
Hue   94

I

Image file formats
    GIF   50
    JPEG   50
    PNG   50
    Proprietary formats   50
    TIFF   50
Image menu.   See Menu bar: Image
Images
    Obtaining   28
    Saving
        Save As command   50, 130
Image size   102
Import button   28
Importing images   28-29
    From files and folders   28
Info panel.   See Panels: Info
Interpolation   104

J

Joining points
  For a selection   108
JPEG   50
  For merging layers   83

L

Lasso tools   108-109
Layer menu.   See Menu bar: Layer
Layers
  Adding   122
  Adjustment layers   123-124
  Background layer   121
  Deleting   125
  File size   130
  Fill layers   123-124
  Flattening images   130
  Hiding   125
  Layer Masks   126-128
  Locking   125
  Moving   125
  Opacity   129
  Overview   120
  Preserving   130
  Saving   130
Layers panel   121.   See also Panels: Layers
Levels
  Adjusting manually   98-99
Lines
  Adding   145
Lomo Camera Effect.
       See Camera Effects: Lomo Camera Effect
Looking for people   36-37

M

Mac.   See Elements: For the Mac
Magic Wand tool   110
Magnification
  Increasing/decreasing   66
  Navigator panel   67
  View menu   66
  Zoom tool   66
Marquee tools   107

Media View   20, 30-33
  Accessing images   31
  Captions   33
  Information panel   33
  Tags panel   32
  Taskbar   32
Megapixels   102
Memory card   34
Menu bar   18
  Edit   18
  Enhance   18
  File   18
  Filter   18
  Help   18
  Image   18
  Layer   18
  Select   18
  View   18
  Window   18
Mobile sharing   170-172
Moving subjects   74-75
Multiple editing effects   78

N

Navigator panel.   See Panels: Navigator
Negatives
  Digital   100

O

Objects
  Adding   141
Obtaining images   28
  From a pen drive   29
Online printing   185
Online resources
  Downloading   150, 174
Opacity   124
Opening images   50
Open Recently Edited File command   50
Organizer workspace   20
Orton Effect.   See Camera Effects: Orton Effect
Out of Bounds.   See Photo Play effects: Out of Bounds
Outside a main image   160-163

P

Paint Bucket tool	142
Panel Bin	16
Panels	16
Actions	16
Adjustments	16
Color Swatches	16
Effects	16
Favorites	16
Graphics	16
Histogram	16
History	16
Info	16
Layers	16
Navigator	16, 67
Working with	17
Panoramas	
Capturing images for	90
Clean Edges	
For filling edges	92
Color correction	92
Creating	90-92
Cropping	92
Possible subjects	91
Pattern cloning	61
PDF	186
Pencil tool	145
Pen drive	29
People recognition	36-37
People View	21, 36-37
Perfect Portrait option	70
Pet eye.	See Red-eye: Pet red-eye
Photo Bin	11
Photo Downloader	28
Photo Editor workspace	10
Photo Effects	154, 163
Photomerge Compose	
See Photomerge effects: Compose	
Photomerge effects	86-87
Compose	86, 88-89
Exposure	86
Faces	86
Group Shot	87
Panorama	87
Scene Cleaner	87
Photo Play effects	
Out of Bounds	160-163
Photo Puzzles	158-159
Reflections	164-166
Photo Puzzles. See Photo Play effects: Photo Puzzles	
Photoshop	8
Photoshop PDD	50

For preserving layers	83
Photoshop PSD	50
For preserving layers	83
Pixels	102
Pixels per inch	
For printing	180
Places View	21, 38-39
PNG	50
Portable Document Format.	See PDF
Portraits	115
PPI.	See Pixels per inch
Preferences	19
Display & Cursors	19
General	19
Guides & Grid	19
Organize & Share	19
Performance	19
Plug-Ins	19
Saving Files	19
Transparency	19
Type	19
Units & Rulers	19
Premiere.	See Elements Premiere
Previewing editing effects	55
Printing	
Borderless printing	183
On a local printer	181
Photo prints	181
Resampling images	180
Print Layouts	183-184
Contact Sheets	184
Picture Package	183
Print options	181
Print settings	182
Print size	180-181
Projects	
Overview	173-174

Q

Quick edit mode	10, 12, 78-81
Adjustments	78, 80-81
Balance panel	81
Color panel	81
Effects	82
Enhancing photos	82
Exposure panel	80
Frames	83
Lighting panel	80
Sharpen panel	81
Smart Fix panel	80
Textures	83

Toolbox   79
  Crop tool   79
  Hand tool   79
  Move tool   79
  Quick Selection tool   79
  Red-eye Removal tool   79
  Spot Healing/Healing tool   79
  Text tool   79
  Whiten Teeth tool   79
  Zoom tool   79
Using   78

R

RAW images
  Working with Elements   100-101
Recoloring areas
  With the Gradient tool   143
  With the Paint Bucket tool   142
Red-eye
  Avoiding   70
  Pet red-eye   71
  Removing   70-72
Refine Edge option   117
Reflections.   See Photo Play effects: Reflections
Removing items   72-73
Resampling   104
Resolution
  Image   102
  Print   103
RGB color model   96
Rotating
  Images   64
  Layers   64
Rule of Thirds   58
Rulers   66

S

Saturation   94
Scanner   50
Scratch disk   19
Search box   44
Searching for images
  By object   47
  Duplicate Photos   47
  Multiple searches   46
  Using tags and collections   44
  Visual Similarity   47

Selecting images   31
Selections
  Adding to   114, 118
  Areas of color   110
  Editing   118
  Expanding   118
  Growing   118
  Inverting   114
  Moving   118
  Overview   106
  Refining   116
  Symmetrical   107
  With Lasso tools   108-109
  With Selection Brush tool   111
Select menu.   See Menu bar: Select
Shadows/Highlights.
            See Color enhancements: Shadows/Highlights
Shapes
  Adding   141
Share mode   23
  About   168
  Burn Video DVD/BluRay   168
  Email   168
  Facebook   168
  Flickr   168
  PDF SlideShow   168
  Private Web Album   168
  Twitter   168
  Vimeo   168
  YouTube   168
Sharpening   81
Similar images
  Stacking   34
Skin tone   63
Smartphones   170
Softening portraits   115
Sorting images
  About   20
Stacks   34

T

Tablets   170
Tagging
  Images   42-43
Tagging people.   See People View
Tags
  Adding multiple   43
Taskbar   11
Text
  Adding   132
  Adding to a custom path   136-137

Adding to a selection 134
Adding to a shape 135
Adding to layers 122
Customizing 134-137
Distorting 138
Formatting 132
Text masks 139-140
Thumbnails 20
Tilt-Shift effect 156
Tonal range 97
Toolbox 15
Tool Options panel 11
Tools
Additional options 15
Brush 145
Burn 54
Dodge 54
Eraser 68
Gradient 143-144
Healing Brush 62
Impressionist Brush 146
Lasso 108-109
Magic Wand 110
Magnetic Lasso 109
Marquee 107
Paint Bucket 142
Pattern Stamp 61
Pencil 145
Polygonal Lasso 108
Quick Selection 112
Selection Brush 111
Smart Brush 113
Spot Healing Brush 63
Transforming 65
Distort 65
Free Transform 65
Perspective 65
Skew 65
Transparent backgrounds
Creating 123

U

Unsharp Mask 81

V

Version sets 35
Video
Finding 52
Viewing 52
Working with 51-52
Viewing images
About 20
View menu. See Menu bar: View
Visibility
Using layers 129

W

Watching folders 30
Welcome Screen 9
White balance
In RAW images 100
Whitening teeth 79
Window menu. See Menu bar: Window
Word
Copying text masks to 140

Z

Zoom Burst. See Camera Effects: Zoom Burst
Zooming
On an image 66